Praise for *Weaponized*

In *Weaponized*, Seth Barron argues provocatively and effectively that the Left has burrowed far deeper into the infrastructure of American life than is commonly understood. I've heard few arguments as eye-opening as Barron's connection between suburban upzoning and open borders. *Weaponized* should be read by anyone concerned about the direction of the country and understanding how we arrived here.

—TOM FITTON, president, Judicial Watch

In *Weaponized*, Seth Barron deftly examines the infiltration of major institutions of American life by radical ideologues who seek to transform the national order. Barron offers fresh insights about citizenship, race relations, and education and housing policies to reach surprising conclusions. His lively style and amusing references make for an engaging, enjoyable read. This is essential reading for enlightened citizens alarmed at the current crisis of American constitutionalism.

—RYAN WILLIAMS, president, The Claremont Institute;
publisher, *The Claremont Review of Books*

Weaponized presents, in emphatic but well-reasoned detail, how the new progressivism is undermining society—in race relations, housing, the economy, and education. It provides a superb wake-up call that is sorely needed to combat the outbreak of insanity that threatens us all. It is essential reading not just for conservatives, but perhaps even more so for independents and remaining rational Democrats.

—JOEL KOTKIN, presidential fellow in Urban Futures,
Chapman University; author, *The Coming of Neo-Feudalism*

Seth Barron's new book *Weaponized* is a trenchant, lively examination of the liberal "long march through the institutions" of American life. I don't often read a book that combines policy analysis with deft wit but Seth pulls it off. He traces the anticarceral Third Worldism of Zohran Mamdani to its philosophical origins and unveils Angela Davis as the secret sharer of the contemporary left. *Weaponized* is a must-read for anyone who hungers to comprehend the extent to which contemporary progressivism has upended the world.

—JOHN TIERNEY, author, *The Power of Bad*

Does America have a "housing crisis," outweighing existing residents' right to have some say over what their neighborhoods look like? Is America a "nation of immigrants," meaning that any questioning of an open border is xenophobic? Are highways "racist"? Are police departments the legacy of our "original sin" of slavery? In *Weaponized*, Seth Barron carefully and incisively reasons his way through the seemingly unimpeachable shibboleths by which the left would govern us.

—NICOLE GELINAS, senior fellow, Manhattan Institute; author, *Movement: New York's Long War to Take Back Its Streets from the Car*

Many of us feel that we've been living through an era of rapid and disorienting change. Institutions we once relied on to maintain the social order have become instruments of instability. Seth Barron explains the disturbing strategies behind this "weaponization" of American institutions. He does so with wit and an unerring touch for the illustrative detail. An essential chronicle of social conditions and public administration in 2020s America.

—STEPHEN EIDE, senior fellow, Manhattan Institute; author, *Homelessness in America: The History and Tragedy of an Intractable Social Problem*

WEAPONIZED

WEAPONIZED

THE LEFT'S CAPTURE *and* DESTRUCTION *of* AMERICA'S SACRED INSTITUTIONS

SETH BARRON

Humanix Books
www.humanixbooks.com

To M. and J.

CONTENTS

LAND ACKNOWLEDGMENT

I'd like to begin by noting that this book was conceived, contracted, and composed upon the island of Manhattan, which was sold, ceded, and surrendered by the native Lenape to Peter Minuit in 1626, exactly 400 years ago.

I acknowledge and honor the many settlers, colonists, laborers, and merchants who pacified, civilized, and capitalized this city of my birth and that of my parents, wife, and children.

New York City was the first capital of the United States, and despite its recent socio-political collapse, one has strong hopes that the city will rise again and prove worthy of its magnificent history.

AUTHOR'S
NOTE

Elections are like pond iridescence, a thin, entrancing second-ary effect of the anaerobic processing of sludge. But they are a handy way to think about history. Any analysis of American political culture necessarily refers to presidential terms as eras for the sake of narrative coherence. And it makes sense, because "elections have consequences," as Barack Obama reminded John McCain. When Biden took over the White House in 2021, he (or, more likely, anonymous operatives) immediately imposed a radical "whole of government" implementation of the hard-left equalitarian, pro-trans, pro-DEI, open-borders agenda.

That happened. And when Trump took back the White House in 2025, he rolled back many of Biden's actions. He closed the border, eliminated DEI requirements in hiring, pulled fund-ing and support for transgender propaganda and inclusion in the military and education, and imposed his own set of "whole of government" initiatives.

So, is that it? Is American life defined by which party won the last election?

Kind of, obviously, but the pond has depths.

Society is defined by its institutions, broad systems, or apparatuses that govern how we live. These institutions are informed by shared norms and values and represent an implicit mutual agreement among members of a society that things are run one way and not another. In this book, I am looking at four institutions—citizenship, policing, housing, and education—each of which defines social existence in the same essential, invisible way that fish live in water.

Controlling the operation of these institutions is key to controlling the country and is why politics are so important.

So, the point of this book really is to look under the hoods of these apparatuses, get a sense of how they work politically, and, hopefully, explain how the Left has already warped the American way of life to the point where it may be unrecognizable, if not unrecoverable.

Seth Barron

INTRODUCTION

We have heard a lot about "weaponization" over the last few years. On social media, it has become a kind of shorthand, like the word "gaslighting," for anything that someone finds annoying or unscrupulous.

For instance, it is common among relationship counselors or observers of the dynamics between men and women to talk about "weaponized incompetence." This phrase usually refers to men pretending not to understand how to handle young children or the complexities of meal prep to get out of doing housework. Men have used their alleged inability to do things as a defensive weapon in their war with women.

Or you might hear about "weaponized intimacy," which occurs when someone withholds love or sex to get their partner to do what they want—such as, I guess, meal prep or taking care of the kids.

These are interesting phenomena, but my intention in this book is less to talk about weaponization in the sense of interpersonal relations and more about the core meaning of the term as it relates to the contemporary political scene. In America today, weaponization refers to the use of ostensibly neutral institutions or concepts for political or ideological ends that would be difficult to achieve without leveraging the good reputation of those institutions.

It is common, for instance, to hear about "the politics of cruelty," the title of a 1994 book by feminist Kate Millet. Millet's book was about the use of torture by authoritarian regimes, but the term has been repurposed to characterize conservative policies as cruel. Work requirements for food stamps or making public benches difficult to sleep on are examples of the politics of cruelty.

But I am more interested in, for instance, the ways that immigration—a process that Americans generally look kindly on—has been made a tool for the disruption of American political life, the suppression of wages, and the eradication of American cultural memory. Citizenship has been devalued, weaponized, and turned against the citizens of the country, who are told in so many words that their time at the helm is over.

Policing, which historically has maintained a high reputation among the public, has been systematically and tendentiously tied to the legacy of slavery and a narrative of global oppression in order to disrupt public order, allocate tax dollars to "community based" radical social-service nonprofit organizations, and ultimately further an agenda of destruction of Western values and society.

Owning a home is central to the American identity, and people dream of possessing space—extra rooms, wide lawns, capacious garages—as tiny symbols of the American frontier. But private homeownership is at the root of everything wrong with modern society to the Left, which wishes to verticalize housing in the form of dense, forcibly integrated complexes proximate to mass transit. Local zoning laws are being systematically dismantled in state legislatures in order to impose densification upon the American people.

Education is the great cultural equalizer. The lessons of grade school, the embarrassment of junior high, and the coming-of-age rituals of high school bind Americans with a shared process of socialization that, good or bad, offers a common register of experience. But public education has been captured by teachers unions, "educrats," and leftist activists who have turned schools into indoctrination camps for progressive nostrums.

This is not a new phenomenon, certainly. The history of war is the history of exploiting sentiments to convince the population to sacrifice its children to a greater cause. Governments play on love of country, or religion, or xenophobia to get the people to act collectively.

In 1898, the explosion of the U.S.S. *Maine* in Havana Harbor became a pretext for war with Spain, which was blamed for blowing up an American battleship, though the explosion was likely caused by a fire in the ship's coal bunker. The government, assisted by the tabloid press of the day, agitated the public to the point where they were enthusiastic about seizing Cuba and Guam.

In 1964, President Lyndon Johnson lied about an attack on a U.S. warship in the Gulf of Tonkin by North Vietnam to secure congressional authorization to step up American military operations in Indochina. In 1983, Ronald Reagan ordered the invasion of the tiny island nation of Grenada and overthrew the Marxist prime minister. This intervention came two days after terror faction Islamic Jihad blew up truck bombs in Beirut, killing hundreds of U.S. Marines.

Critics noted that the Grenada spectacle was probably an effort to deflect attention from the bad news in Lebanon, promoting instead a glorious military triumph. There are thousands of examples of this sort of thing. Governments lie or manipulate us all the time, and this use of power to persuade the people is a form of weaponization.

In the 1990s, independent counsel Ken Starr was tasked with investigating corruption surrounding President Bill Clinton and his business interests from the years when he was governor of Arkansas. Starr's remit became somewhat wide and free-wheeling, eventually involving the totally unrelated sexual relationship between Clinton and Monica Lewinsky, a young intern in his office. Though Lewinsky was inarguably the subordinate in this office romance, the Democrat-dominated media went along with the White House line that she was a domineering hussy who had entrapped the president. The ensuing scandal and impeachment of Clinton for lying under oath were condemned as the "criminalization of politics."

This term caught on and was used in the George W. Bush years, too, to describe various investigations and scandals. Republicans dismissed the Plame Affair—which involved the leaking of a CIA agent's name in connection with fallout surrounding the promised "weapons of mass destruction" that were never found in Iraq but had served as the reason for going to war in the first place—as more "criminalization of politics."

In both these cases, the argument was that normal political activity—presidents having sex with young interns, officials lying to Congress—was now being scrutinized unfairly, or even weaponized.

But in recent years, Americans have been treated to the spectacle of one of the most open and blatant forms of weaponization imaginable, namely the use of law enforcement and the judicial system in the relentless prosecution of Donald Trump and anyone associated with him.

The period from 2021 to 2025 will be seen historically as an *interregnum*, a discontinuity or interruption of normal government, kind of like England between the execution of King Charles I and the resumption of the monarchy a decade later by his son, King Charles II. Or, if you want to look at it through the opposite end of the telescope, kind of like how the Democrats behaved after Trump was defeated in 2020. Biden's victory was seen by the media and conventional power structure as a return to normalcy, and the Trump years as an anomaly that almost cratered American democracy.

Whatever you believe about the 2020 election, it was certainly marked by irregularities. Numerous secretaries of state, citing the pandemic, unilaterally made changes to the "Times, Places and Manner of holding Elections" that are constitutionally assigned specifically to state legislatures. These changes were subtle but significant, such as loosening the standards by which signatures on mail-in ballots are checked, or mass-mailing ballots to all registered voters. These changes created room for abuse.

Even if there was probably no actual effort to "steal" the election through ballot fraud, the fact that news favorable to the Trump campaign—for instance, regarding Hunter Biden's laptop and the information it contained about alleged Biden family corruption—was actively suppressed by the mass media, in conjunction with corrupt elements of the "intelligence community," should be enough to raise questions about its fairness.

But even assuming the Biden presidency was legally installed, it conducted itself like a usurping regime. In the same way that plotters of a successful coup will murder the deposed leader, engage in mass repression, and stage show trials in order to document the alleged crimes of the previous government, the Biden administration set about methodically promoting the idea that Trump's presidency had been a criminal conspiracy from top to bottom.

In an effort to destroy Trump and sow the ground of the MAGA movement with salt that it would remain barren forever, Democrats brought civil and criminal charges against him and his family, in a variety of jurisdictions, and at multiple levels of government. They sought to humiliate and bankrupt him. They changed New York State law specifically to facilitate a lawsuit about an alleged sexual assault from decades earlier.

The FBI stormed into Trump's house to seek stray documents that the former president had allegedly, and preposterously, stolen. The Biden administration conspired with the New York state attorney general to concoct a mortgage fraud case that was based on neither a complaint nor undue financial gain. The regime tore through internal documents of the Trump organization to develop a tendentious criminal case based on how certain payments had been booked in the company's private files.

Dozens of associates of Donald Trump were investigated, arrested, indicted, and, in some cases, convicted and jailed for crimes that existed only because law enforcement had gone looking for them. Biden's Department of Justice spent millions of dollars tracking down, arresting, and prosecuting more than a thousand people who had entered the U.S. Capitol on January 6, 2021. Citizens who had committed no violence, and who had, in fact, been ushered into the building by police officers, received substantial sentences in federal prison. Some were kept in solitary confinement, others hounded out of their careers and subjected to years of harassment by federal officials across the government.

There has been, and there will be, much written about the ways in which the FBI, the Obama White House, the "intelligence community," and sneaky elements of the media and legal profession conspired in 2016 to destroy Trump's candidacy. And following the shock of Hillary Clinton's defeat, they set about weaponizing the "Deep State"—the unelected powers that run the country behind the scenes—to destroy his presidency.

This is not that book, but it is closely related. This book examines the weaponization of certain key institutions by the Left in order to impose its agenda upon the American people. I examine four domains that broadly define American life—citizenship, policing, education, and housing—and demonstrate their capture by radical forces that seek to interrupt, distort, and heave up the American way of life.

WEAPONIZED

ONE

CITIZENSHIP

Coming to America . . . to Shoot Sea Lions

Democrat Congresswoman Yvette Clarke made a telling gaffe early in 2024, while New York City was grappling with the weekly arrival of thousands of migrants seeking free shelter, food, healthcare, and cash outlays. "In Brooklyn," explained the congresswoman, "we have a diaspora that can absorb a significant number of these migrants. . . . I need more people in my district just for redistricting purposes!"[1]

That is, Representative Clarke wants more people in her district to bloat the local count in an era of declining population; New York State has lost congressional seats every decade since 1950 due to reapportionment, and there's no telling what Brooklyn may look like after 2030. New York State's population, after all, is not just declining in relation to other states; the number of New Yorkers is going down.

In our system, the U.S. Census enumerates the gross population of the country to determine how the congressional seats are assigned. Noncitizens are counted for these purposes, which means that politicians like Yvette Clarke are happy to cram nonvoting illegal aliens into her district. They fill out the numbers and allow her to demand more resources for her crowded district.

The fact that the residents of her district *can't* vote is a plus for Clarke and other Democrat politicians who represent zones of massive illegal alien density. These districts resemble the "rotten boroughs" of Britain before the Reform Act of 1832. The boundaries of these boroughs had been defined perhaps centuries before and often encompassed grand private estates where the residents were tenants of or dependent on the major local landowner. The British Parliament was lopsidedly composed of legislators who had been elected by as few as a half-dozen voters.

During the Biden years, when millions of illegal aliens streamed into the country, Republicans and other critics of the open border policy hypothesized that its real purpose was to bring in fresh Democrat voters. These newly arrived migrants can't vote legally—at least not immediately—but the larger point is valid. Mass immigration to blue states like California and New York, where the populations are in decline, is an effective way to plug the drain of people running for the exits to escape the combination of high taxes, governmental incompetence, and low quality of life that increasingly defines states run according to outdated progressive principles.

The problem, of course, predated the Biden administration. In July of 2015, a young woman was walking along the popular, touristy Embarcadero waterfront in San Francisco with her dad and a friend, taking in the sights and sounds of the famous bay, when she was shot in the back. She died a few hours later, in the hospital.

José Inez García Zárate, the man who shot and killed 32-year-old Kate Steinle, was an illegal immigrant who had been deported from the United States on five separate occasions. The history of his peregrinations makes for some colorful reading.

It's unclear when he first came to America, but in 1991 García Zárate was arrested and convicted of drug charges in Arizona. Over the next few years, he was convicted of three more felony drug charges in the state of Washington, including the manufacture of narcotics. He was deported in 1994 but came back and was again convicted of drug possession in Washington. He was deported again in 1997 and then for a third time in 1998. He served five years in federal prison for having re-entered the country and was deported in 2003 upon his release.[2]

You'd think four deportations and even more felony convictions, following a lengthy stint in prison, might've convinced García Zárate to try his luck at home in Mexico. After all, his personal American Dream wasn't amounting to a lot that he couldn't accomplish anywhere else. You don't have to be in the United States to be a drug dealer or make and use methamphetamine. But the lure of America called him back, evidently, as he was arrested for illegal entry again and deported for the fifth time in 2009.

In March of 2015, the San Francisco Sheriff's Office, which had an old warrant out for García Zárate's arrest, became aware that he was in federal custody in San Bernardino. The Bureau of Prisons transferred García Zárate to the sheriff, who was notified that Immigration and Customs Enforcement (ICE) wanted García Zárate detained upon release, as they wished to deport him—again. As it turned out, the district attorney declined to prosecute García Zárate for his outstanding drug trafficking charges, and under local "sanctuary city" law, the sheriff was obligated to refuse any cooperation with ICE. So, a convicted felon, multiple deportee, and illegal alien was set free to try his fortunes in San Francisco—again.

Two months later, García Zárate shot and killed Kate Steinle. He first claimed that he had merely been shooting at sea lions with a gun he had found under a bench, but later insisted the gun had spontaneously gone off as he had been unwrapping it from the T-shirt he had found it bound in.

The case of Kate Steinle horrified many around the nation. Her death also coincided closely with Donald Trump's announcement that he planned to run for president on a platform of national greatness, which would include building a "great, great wall" between the United States and Mexico, with the aim of plugging a hole that had made America a "dumping ground for the world's problems."

Trump's speech, delivered in the atrium of his eponymous Fifth Avenue pleasure dome, essentially laid out the basis for his contentious campaign and a presidency that exposed major divisions in American politics. He planned, in words that drove his opponents mad, to "make this country great again," and he would do it by centering America's interests around those of the nation and its people.

> When Mexico sends its people, they're not sending their best. They're not sending you. They're sending people that have lots of problems, and they're bringing those problems to us. They're bringing drugs. They're bringing crime. They're rapists. And some, I assume, are good people.
>
> But I speak to border guards and they tell us what we're getting. And it only makes common sense. It only makes common sense. They're sending us not the right people.[3]

It's hard to overstate the impact of this speech, and it's bizarre to consider that it was the kickoff address to a longshot presidential campaign—by any standard the most unusual in U.S. history—that ended in a victory that stunned the world. Trump's comments delighted and horrified people in almost equal measure. Americans who had watched for years as a bipartisan consensus in Washington enabled the flow of illegal immigration, and blocked effective enforcement of the law, were thrilled to hear a candidate for high office address the question with the gravity they believed it deserved.

On the other side, advocates for cheap labor and Democrat enthusiasts of the "browning of America"—a phrase that entered American discourse in 1990 when *Time* ran a celebratory issue on the subject—jumped to denounce Trump for his alleged racism in calling Mexican illegal aliens—and all Latinos, by extension—"rapists." Though the meaning of his speech was reasonably clear—that, among the millions of people illegally crossing the border, some were unquestionably "bad hombres"—the mainstream media immediately cast his comments in the worst possible light. In the ten years since he made that speech, it has been reliably reported and repeated that Trump thinks Hispanics (or maybe just Hispanic men) are rapists.

In a divided political culture, everything that happens winds up on one or the other side of the Trump split. Does the other side question the efficacy of masks to prevent the spread of Covid? Then we will embrace masking. Did Trump advise pregnant women to avoid taking Tylenol? Then Trump-hating pregnant women around the country will swallow an extra dose or two. The killing of Katie Steinle fed into this perverse calculus, too. When Trump drew attention to her death at the apparent hands of an oft-deported repeat felon, who happened to be Mexican, José Inez García Zárate became a celebrated cause. Six weeks after Steinle's death, the *New*

York Times printed an editorial that sympathetically referred to García Zárate as a "troubled immigrant," who "has become the dark-skinned face of the Mexican killers that Donald Trump—in a racist speech announcing his presidential campaign, and numerous interviews thereafter—has been warning the nation about."

Trump's comments on the case turned the trial of Steinle's killer into a kind of referendum on illegal immigration, sanctuary cities, and enforcement of the law, and turned García Zárate into a martyr for the cause. The *Times* blamed "right-wing commenters and politicians, shamelessly willing to scapegoat 11 million unauthorized immigrants as a criminal class and national-security threat," and insisted that it would have been "unconstitutional" for San Francisco to hold García Zárate for deportation proceedings, though courts have upheld the practice.[4]

García Zárate's trial for the murder of Kate Steinle ended in a bizarre acquittal on all major counts: first-degree murder, second-degree murder, and involuntary manslaughter. Observers around the nation, and not just conservatives, were stunned. How could a known criminal, who claimed he had been idly shooting at sea lions, indisputably fire the bullet that killed a tourist, yet face zero consequences for her death? True, he was found guilty of being a felon in possession of a firearm—though even that conviction was overturned on appeal. The Department of Justice filed federal gun charges against García Zárate, and that conviction stuck.

To what extent did the political valence around the issue of illegal immigration, and Donald Trump's foregrounding of the question in his presidential campaign, lubricate the skids and allow García Zárate to evade justice for his crime? Was there bias among the jurors against the prosecution of an illegal immigrant, simply because Trump had made an issue of Kate Steinle's killing?

It's impossible to say that the question can be clearly answered. San Francisco is famously liberal and "tolerant" to a fault. It had been a "sanctuary city" since 1989, and in 2013 it passed its "Due Process for All" law, which prevented the city from even giving ICE a heads-up that it was releasing a dangerous illegal alien from local jail. If any city in America might perversely give a lifetime loser like García Zárate a seventh or eighth chance, San Francisco would be the place.

But local reporting indicates otherwise. An alternate juror in the case, who had attended the entire trial, responded to national disbelief at the verdict by insisting in *Politico* that "the jury was right to make the decision that it did." A mechanical engineer by profession, Phil Van Stockum explained that the evidence in the case made it difficult to understand how a first-degree (intentional) murder charge could have held up. But even he, totally sympathetic to the jurors' decision and, implicitly, to the case of "Jose Ines García Zárate, the undocumented immigrant who was accused of killing Steinle," seemed somewhat baffled as to how the jury found García Zárate not guilty of manslaughter. "But why the manslaughter acquittal? Most of the confusion I've encountered has been over this part of the verdict, and it does seem to me personally that manslaughter is the appropriate charge for Steinle's killing."[5]

Van Stockum was unable to offer much in the way of explanation for why the jury had acquitted García Zárate of committing involuntary manslaughter—the obvious verdict. But attorney Francisco Ugarte, who ran the immigration division at the San Francisco Public Defender's Office, had no doubt about the essential innocence of his client and the reasons for his prosecution. "Nothing about Mr. García Zárate's ethnicity, nothing about his immigration status, nothing about the fact that he is born in Mexico had any relevance as to what happened on July 1, 2015," Ugarte said.

Well, in fact that's not quite true: He came to America illegally from Mexico on multiple occasions, was deported, and was free to "find" stolen guns and fire them at sea lions, only because San

Francisco had made the perverse choice to prioritize the rights of illegal immigrants over the safety of legal residents and citizens.[6]

The case of García Zárate wasn't unique. Throughout the country, people opposed to Donald Trump's border security agenda turned out by the thousands to protest the deportation of convicted felons. Removing criminal aliens to their countries of origin was described as not merely an outrage but unspeakable brutality. The same situation is being repeated in Trump's second term, as mobs attack ICE agents arresting criminal aliens in major cities and insist that the arrestees are being "kidnapped" and "disappeared."

In 2020, the *New York Times* ran an opinion piece imploring then-governor Andrew Cuomo to pardon Tyrone Abraham, whose "story shows what happens when a state's criminal justice system collides with federal immigration enforcement." A native of Jamaica who had received permanent residency when he moved to the U.S. at age 11, Abraham spent 25 years in prison for murdering a rival drug dealer. As he explained it to the left-wing prison abolitionist Marshall Project:

> I was also involved with two women at the same time. Both were pregnant by my senior year. My job at a fast food restaurant wasn't enough to support children, so with a little convincing from friends, I dropped out of school and started selling drugs. When my mother found out what I was doing, I left home in shame. My girlfriend and I started living in a broken car that belonged to a friend.
>
> On June 23, 1992—two months before my first child was born—an older, bigger dealer ordered me to stop selling in the same building as him. When I ignored him, he smacked me in the face. I left the area, but later when I came back to see my girlfriend, I encountered him again. He assaulted

me and blocked my exit. That's when I went and got a gun a friend was holding for me and fatally shot him.[7]

Caught between two lovers, humiliated by an older drug dealer, Tyrone Abraham was put in a familiar quandary for new dads, and had to murder the man who had slapped him in the face. In the end, Abraham was paroled but still faced the threat of deportation to Jamaica; Cuomo gave him a last-minute pardon, allowing him to stay in America.

The principle that law enforcement should prioritize the minimization of consequences to illegal immigrant offenders is widely held among prosecutors and advocates on the Left. When San Francisco district attorney Chesa Boudin—scion of one of the most illustrious leftist American families—confronted the issue of the fentanyl epidemic in his city in 2020, he cautioned against acting too rashly in arresting the pushers of the deadly drug.

"A significant percentage of people selling drugs in San Francisco, perhaps as many as half, are from Honduras," explained District Attorney Boudin, "We need to be mindful of the impact our interventions have. Some of them have family members in Honduras who have been or will be harmed if they don't continue to pay off the traffickers who brought them here."[8]

In other words, drug dealers have families, too. We must make sure that the cartels that might kill the drug dealers' families if they don't receive their money get paid. The fact that around 55,000 Americans die annually from opioid overdoses[9]— down from 80,000 in 2020—must be balanced against the fact that Hondurans in the United States send almost a billion dollars home each year in the form of remittances, which is second only to coffee exports as a source of foreign income.

In New York City, a Trinidadian mortgage fraudster named Ravi Ragbir, who had spent time in federal prison, lived for 12 years under an order of removal, which he managed to delay. In the meantime, he became the director of a group called the New Sanctuary Coalition, the main purpose of which appears to have been to defend his case.

When ICE took Ragbir into custody to deport him in 2018, New York City's political class took to the streets, blocking traffic, including an ambulance. Elected officials scuffled with police and demanded his immediate freedom. Federal district court judge Katherine B. Forrest declared that ICE, in detaining Ragbir at his "check-in" appointment, had violated his fictional constitutional "freedom to say goodbye," though he had been ordered to leave the country in 2006—ample time to get hugs and kisses.[10]

Removing a convicted criminal and sending him home—to Trinidad, a democratic, prosperous country where English is the primary language and from which Ravi Ragbir had emigrated as an adult—is standard practice in every functioning society in the world. But advocates for the rights of immigrants represented — and continue to represent—such repatriation as a human rights violation on par with the worst forms of human savagery.

Brooklyn Congresswoman Yvette Clarke declared at an anti-ICE protest that "we are standing in front of a building that has become the headquarters for the Gestapo of the United States of America." The Gestapo was the secret police of Nazi Germany, routinely torturing and killing enemies of the state. ICE is not credibly accused of any such excesses. The New Jersey ACLU tweeted that Judge Forrest's invention of a right to say goodbye at a time and manner of a deportee's choosing "affirmed the Constitution, saying we are not the kind of country that whisks people away and disappears them." When evil, corrupt governments "disappear" people, they throw them out of helicopters offshore or dissolve their corpses in acid. Ravi Ragbir was going to be sent to the nation of his birth, the passport of which he still held.

In the end, things worked out for Ravi. He got his deportation stayed and later was the recipient of one of President Biden's controversial and dubious last-minute pardons. Congresswoman Clarke put out a press release enthusing, "As Mr. Ragbir begins his next chapter, free from persecution and free to continue the critical work that has improved the lives of countless individuals and families in this country, I look forward to witnessing the new heights he can achieve unburdened by this hardship that has too long loomed above his head. I thank him for his service to our nation's most vulnerable communities, and I pledge to always stand at his side and the side of our immigrant neighbors when injustice threatens their American Dream."[11]

Ravi Ragbir's "persecution," in the words of the congresswoman, was to face immigration consequences for having been convicted of mortgage fraud. It's worth noting that Trinidad has been engulfed by Venezuelans fleeing socialist immiseration, and the island nation has responded by deporting those migrants whose claims for refugee status were found wanting.

"The Government's policy is quite clear," explained Trinidad's Minister of National Security Fitzgerald Hinds. "We have made arrangements to host all of those Venezuelans who registered in our Migrant Registration Framework, and to allow them to work and enjoy the protection of the laws and Constitution of Trinidad and Tobago. But, where persons are found outside of this framework, and/or otherwise outside of the purview of the Immigration Act of Trinidad and Tobago; or any other criminal laws, they will not enjoy such protection."[12]

Judge Forrest's invention of the right to say good-bye bore significant resemblance to the rulings of Judge Derrick Watson, chief judge of the U.S. District Court in Hawaii. Almost immediately upon taking office as president in January 2017, Donald Trump made good on a key campaign promise by suspending travel from a handful of nations identified as sources of terrorism. These nations—Iran, Iraq, Libya, Somalia, Sudan, Syria, and Yemen—are all majority-Muslim, and activists immediately started calling the visa restriction program the "Muslim Ban."

Reaction was intense. Thousands of activists, including lawyers, flooded airports to protest and offer representation to excluded persons. Crowds chanted, "No hate, no fear/Everyone is welcome here!" and "No Trump! No KKK! No fascist USA!" to express their dismay at the ban. At JFK Airport in New York, congressional representatives Jerold Nadler and Nydia Velazquez demanded access to an Iraqi holder of a visa who had been detained by immigration officials. Nadler called Trump's order "discriminatory and disgusting."

In California, then-senator Kamala Harris said she was especially horrified at the timing of Trump's executive order. "On Holocaust Memorial Day, President Trump enacted an executive order that will restrict refugees from Muslim-majority countries," explained the senator and future vice president, drawing an implicit connection between a 90-day ban on travel from seven countries, and a 120-day suspension of refugee resettlement, and the industrial-scale murder of 11 million people in Nazi death camps. "We can't turn our backs on the millions of refugees who are contributing to our country and our economy," continued Harris. "During the Holocaust, we failed to let refugees like Anne Frank into our country. We can't let history repeat itself."[13]

It's worth noting that the United States admitted around a quarter of a million European refugees between 1933 and 1945, at a time the American population was about one-third the size it is now, and in the middle of a massive economic depression. The United States Holocaust Memorial Museum notes that "the United States accepted more refugees fleeing Nazi persecution than any other country in the world. Most of these refugees were

Jewish and from central and western Europe." And while Anne
Frank's family did apply for a visa to emigrate to America when
the Germans invaded Holland, the U.S. consulate in Rotterdam
was destroyed in the German bombing of the Dutch port city,
and the visa application was never processed.

Comparisons of the executive order to genocide, apartheid,
and segregation abounded, setting a rhetorical pattern for how
the "#Resistance" responded to virtually everything that Donald
Trump said or did for the next four years. Amidst the furor, few
noticed that Trump's "ban" was based on a list of countries sin-
gled out for enhanced travel restrictions compiled by the previous administration.

In December 2015, then-president Barack Obama signed the
Visa Waiver Program Improvement and Terrorist Travel Prevention
Act, which removed citizens of Iran, Iraq, Libya, Somalia, Sudan,
Syria, and Yemen—the same countries named in Trump's executive
order—from the visa waiver program. The Obama White House
had evidently seen cause to keep a close eye on visitors from those
countries, yet there were no mass demonstrations or accusations
of human rights violations from top elected officials.

Lawsuits were filed around the country on behalf of various
green card holders or previously visaed citizens of Yemen or Sudan
who were stopped at airports, and some of them were admitted in
due course. But activist lawyers carefully shopped their big cases to
the most favorable judicial districts, landing ultimately in Hawaii.
Judge Derrick Watson issued a series of injunctions against
Trump's travel restrictions—and he applied them to the entire
nation. Many were puzzled by this move: How could one federal
judge in a geographically remote area overrule the president, especially on a matter pertaining to borders and national security?

Nationwide injunctions by district court judges are a relative
novelty in American law. Before the 1960s, they were basically

unheard of, and their rise is connected to the surge in judicial activism that began after the passage of civil rights legislation at the same time. Federal civil rights laws, while arguably necessary at the time in order to ensure that black Americans received due process and equal protection under law, instituted a new system of control over society, one that coexists and conflicts with the traditional American understanding of individual liberty. The civil rights regime empowers courts to dictate not just how to interpret law but also how to apply it, down to the minutest level of specificity.

Under this new system of jurisprudence, judges are virtually encouraged to legislate from the bench, creating new laws and rights, and ordering institutions to comply operationally with their dictates. With equality on the basis of race, sex, national origin, and other "protected classes" now at the center of America's new constitutional order, judges could set policy on hiring, promotion, zoning, and virtually any area of life that involves the distribution of goods and opportunities across demographic categories.

Judge Derrick Watson stepped into the debate about Trump's "travel ban" (which mostly just suspended travel for a few months and was never a "ban" in a real sense) and ruled that it could not take effect, anywhere. He based his decision largely on the grounds that, because Trump had tweeted about immigration from Muslim countries, it was clear that the executive orders were rooted in "animus" toward Islam.

Judge Watson gave "standing" (the right to sue) to Ismail Elshikh, a local religious leader of the Muslim community in Hawaii. According to Elshikh, his five children, all U.S. citizens, were "deeply affected" by the ban because it would impact people of their ethnicity and religion overseas. This affinity, according to Elshikh in an argument that Watson accepted, created significant harm and justified blocking Trump's executive order nationwide.

Elshikh also said that the ban had "a direct personal effect" on his children because it might interfere with his mother-in-law's plan to visit Hawaii and meet two of her grandchildren for the first time; she hadn't seen her son since 2005. Furthermore, Elshikh argued that many members of his mosque "have friends and family still living in the countries affected by the travel ban." As long as it remains in effect, "these individuals live in forced separation from those family members and friends."

The argument that a sitting president of the United States should be restrained from his constitutional mandate to protect the nation because a Syrian grandmother might want to visit every 12 years, or because U.S. residents are living in "forced separation" from their friends and family in terrorist-sponsoring nations, sounds weak. But like the arguments put forth by universities that they would be harmed financially if they didn't get to matriculate students from Libya or Yemen, or the argument made in 2019 by a South Texas "community organization" called the Border Network for Human Rights that its "mission" would be impaired if security on the U.S.–Mexico border were increased, these tendentious claims actually formed the basis of judicial opinions that bound the authority of the executive, at least for the year or two that it took for the cases to wind their way to the U.S. Supreme Court, where they were overturned.

The strategy of tying up Trump's border security promises in a thousand gossamer strands of bogus, refracted legal argumentation worked beautifully. Advocates for illegal immigration simply kept challenging the White House in court, shopping their cases to favorable judges, who obliged their ideological allies by blocking Trump's policies and forcing them into the lengthy appeals process. It's ironic that Donald Trump, who was routinely characterized as an authoritarian, fascist dictator, was entirely respectful of the judicial process in this regard. At no point did he ever suggest that he would ignore the ruling of a district court judge, and he always promised to go obediently through the system that was thwarting his mandate.

Fast-forward eight years to the beginning of Trump's second term, and we see the same thing going on. It became clear in early 2025 that the opposition, lacking enough votes in Congress to block Trump's agenda, planned to use the courts to baffle and obstruct virtually every exercise of executive power they didn't like. In the first few months of Trump's term, district court judges lay national injunctions against his efforts to fire federal employees, close down failing federal offices, appoint Elon Musk as the head of the "Department of Government Efficiency," pause payments to certain nonprofit agencies, permit the secretary of the Treasury to consult data kept by his department, cancel Covid-related block grants to the states, and deport criminal illegal aliens. As of this writing, the Supreme Court has finally imposed theoretical limitations on the power of lower courts to issue nationwide injunctions, though the Court permitted various exceptions and loopholes that have not ended the practice.

By the way, it's worth wondering about the power of the courts in our system of separate powers, which are meant to check and balance each other. It's clear how the executive and legislative branches are checked and limited.

But exactly what are the checks on the judiciary, especially if lower court judges are permitted to issue nationwide injunctions that can take many months to resolve on appeal, even if they are clearly partisan and based on the personal opinion of the judges? Judges can be impeached, but that almost never happens unless there is blatant criminality involved. Congress can pass laws regarding the structure of the judicial system, but that is unlikely, too. Basically, we live in a *kritarchy*—rule by judges—restrained only by its fear that it may lose credibility if it goes too far.

WHOSE DREAM IS IT, ANYWAY?

The main point for this discussion, however, is not that the court system has given district court judges the ability to set national policy from the bench but the fact that Judge Watson effectuated so clearly the governing principle regarding immigration and the "national question" in America today. This principle—which Donald Trump violated and for which he was never forgiven nor permitted to govern in a normal way—is that the power to decide who gets to come to America does not belong to the people who live here, nor even to their representatives.

This question touches on something else that is key to American life today. The familiar phrase "the American Dream" was coined or popularized by historian James Truslow Adams in the early 1930s. He described it as "that dream of a land in which life should be better and richer and fuller for everyone, with opportunity for each according to ability or achievement." This sense of opportunity implied social mobility, with succeeding generations ideally improving on the fortunes of their forebears. It meant that a man who broke his back digging ditches or working in a mill might send his sons to high school, and his grandsons to college. But at some point, the American Dream ceased to be something for *Americans* and became spoken of only as something that *foreigners* aspire to. Americans are not entitled to the American Dream. It's only for other people.

In September 2025, the Trump administration announced that it would impose a new $100,000 fee on H-1B visas, which are nonimmigrant work authorizations that allow American companies to hire foreign workers who have specialized skills. These foreign workers are technically permitted to work in the United States for three to six years, and not to the detriment of any American worker, but in reality, the H-1B has become widely abused. Major corporations use H-1B to replace their domestic workforce with foreigners who are tied to their employers for continued sponsorship; and foreigners have figured out elaborate ways to "game" the system in order to gain permanent legal status.

Over the years, Indians have managed to corner the global market on H-1B visa authorization, to the point that 71 percent of all of those visas go to people from India. The new rules led to anger and (understandable) confusion among visa holders and their advocates, some of whom felt betrayed by the country they wanted to move to. "The American dream is officially over," posted popular Indian influencers Abhi & Niyu.[14]

"H-1B visa shake-up crushes the American dream for Indian students," reported NBC News. "Among the top H-1B employers are tech giants such as Amazon, Meta and Google, as well as consulting firms such as Accenture and Deloitte, according to the DHS data. . . . It was a tried and tested formula that held up for decades, enabling what was the Indian dream."[15]

It's certainly easy to comprehend why people in India would want a chance to make a lot of money on top of the possibility of moving to America. They can instantly assume an upper-middle-class life. This is a win-win for the visa holders and the trillion-dollar corporations that hire them, but in what sense is this arrangement beneficial or advantageous to American workers? At the same time that American tech workers are being laid off by the thousand, and college grads who were exhorted to "learn to code" find themselves unable to get hired, trillion-dollar tech companies whine that they need to be able to hire programmers from Asia on the cheap in order to maintain American "competitiveness."

This is the crux of the problem and captures the thesis of this book. Mass immigration has been turned into a weapon directed against the American people. It reduces wages by flooding the labor market. It increases the price of housing. It dislocates community and frays the social fabric. Everyone knows all this, especially the people in power, and that's why they expend so much energy insisting that it's all untrue.

America remains in the grip of forces that seek to remove power from localities and move it upward, either to more remote levels of government or even beyond government into spheres of power where unelected, unaccountable experts decide the fate of the masses. From migration to zoning, from policing to transportation, from education to the conduct of elections, we see a steady effort to remove authority from local, democratic control and insulate decision making among people with expertise who can be trusted to make the right decisions.

The borders of America under Biden were effectively open. Though there is a great body of law regarding legal and illegal entry, permission to work, the procurement of visas, the jeopardy of committing immigration fraud, and deportation, these laws have been enforced irregularly and haphazardly.

For example, a visiting foreigner landing at an international airport is scanned and searched. His biometric identity is established, cross-checked, and matched against international databases. He may be questioned at length about his plans in the country and ordered to unlock his phone and computer and provide total access to all data contained within, on penalty of being sent straight home. If he is carrying documentation regarding his professional credentials while traveling on a tourist visa, he will be quizzed as to his real intentions for entering America. If he doesn't have access to much money or has a criminal record, he may be turned back. If there are discrepancies regarding his visas or documentation that lead to a suspicion of fraud, he may be arrested and either charged or deported with a permanent order of exclusion from America.

Under the Biden border rush, a foreigner who entered the country by walking illegally across the border and surrendering himself to a Border Patrol officer, on the other hand, may or may not have been apprehended. If he claimed that he was seeking asylum based on a "credible fear" of persecution if sent back to his home country, he would likely be given notice of a court date sometime in the next ten years. If he had relatives or friends in the United States, he may have been offered transportation to meet them and settle down. If the entrant had no claim to asylum status and no record of prior deportation, he could be given a court date and then released under the "Alternatives to Detention" (ATD) program. Under the Biden administration, up to 90 percent of illegal migrants who were released under the ATD absconded and remain in the country. Trump's promises of mass deportation of every illegal alien in the country remain scattershot and unlikely to achieve their goal.

The actual number of illegal aliens in America is unknown, but best estimates by the Center for Immigration Studies, which advocates for limited and legal immigration policies, put the figure around 11.5 million as of the beginning of 2022. Of these, approximately 80 percent are native to Latin America. Immigration flows are offset every year by natural morbidity and the fact that many illegal immigrants go home—the fact that the border is porous means that people go back and forth with some regularity. The number was certainly higher under the Biden administration; commentator Ann Coulter suggests the total number of illegal immigrants is likely around 40 million.[16]

Why does the issue of immigration trigger such heated sentiments? It's important to note that immigration has always been a contentious issue in the United States, but that even in the modern era, which has seen a remarkable influx of tens of millions of people—one of the largest waves of migration in human history—there has been almost no significant opposition of the sort that advocates warn about. Warnings that criticism of immigration as a policy will lead to organized violence against immigrants have virtually never been borne out. Countries such as Turkey, the Dominican Republic, South Africa, and Ireland have seen significant anti-migrant violence, but America, aside from isolated incidents, has been remarkably equable about the admission of so many new people.

Despite the tolerant nature of Americans toward newcomers, polls about legal immigration as a policy have consistently shown that Americans are not especially hungry for more of it. Since 1968, the percentage of Americans who would prefer that the level of immigration stay the same or decline has averaged in the high sixties. At no point has more than a third of the polled population favored increased legal immigration, though a large majority of Americans do report that they look favorably on the net contribution of legal immigrants to the country.

The question of illegal immigration reveals much greater opposition. From 2001 through the present, a substantial majority of the population report that they "personally worry about illegal immigration" either a "fair amount" or a "great deal."[17] The percentage of people reporting "a great deal" of worry about illegal immigration spiked in the first two years of the Biden administration to 40 percent, from 32 percent under Trump, as the surge of millions of migrants was permitted to enter the country. In 2021 and 2022, about 80 percent of the population polled reported that large numbers of illegal immigrants entering the country were either a "critical" threat or an "important" threat.

By the end of the Biden administration, it was clear that the American people were no longer willing to abide untrammeled flows of unvetted people crossing the border. In 2024, YouGov reported that 14.6 percent of registered voters called immigration the "most important issue facing the United States,"[18] up from 2.1 percent in 2012. Axios also reported that 55 percent of American adults wanted to see less immigration, the highest number in decades. Biden's erasure of the U.S.–Mexico border was presumably meant to exploit the American people's generous nature and good faith regarding newcomers but appears to have backfired.

Why are people opposed to illegal immigration in particular? For one thing, it violates the sense of fair play and equality that most Americans subscribe to. Despite what many advocates say, the United States is among the most generous countries in the world when it comes to admission of legal immigrants. In fact, one-fifth of all migrants in the entire world live in the United States, and about one million new legal immigrants arrive each year. There is a process involved in moving here, gaining permanent residency, and becoming a citizen, but it is orderly and hardly insurmountable, given that about 800,000 people become American citizens every year through naturalization.

Given that tens of millions of immigrants have followed the rules, it seems unfair for others—largely just because their home country is close by—to jump the line and come here illegally. It has become common among the elite to laugh at life's landlocked losers who whine that "furriners took our jerbs,"[19] but the fact is that Americans at the lower end of the socio-economic scale face direct competition for work and other resources from immigrants—legal and illegal.

This used to be noncontroversial. Organized labor traditionally aligned with immigration restrictionism; the American Federation of Labor backed it in the 1920s, because it was well understood that the forces of capital used surplus labor as a tool to drive down wages. Cesar Chavez, the Chicano founder of the United Farm Workers, viewed illegal immigrants as scabs, opposed laws that would make it easier for migrant workers to get jobs on American farms, and even sent his members to confront illegal aliens at the border.

The period between 1924 and 1965, when America slowed immigration to allow the earlier wave of migrants to assimilate into the American mainstream, coincided with a period of enormous economic expansion and unparalleled prosperity. The spread of unionization in the 1930s was helped by the fact that labor could set terms with capital on an equal basis. The twenty years after World War II were a period when a man with a high-school education and a solid factory job could buy a car and a house and comfortably raise a family.

In 2015, when Bernie Sanders was vying for the Democratic nomination, a reporter suggested that he was in favor of open borders. "Open borders!" he exclaimed. "No, that's a Koch brothers' proposal," he insisted, referring to the billionaire libertarians (one of whom has since died) who favored limited government intervention in markets generally. Bernie Sanders is an old-fashioned socialist who understands how immigration is used to keep labor costs low. It's not a mystery why the *Wall Street Journal*, the chamber of commerce, and the Republican Party donor class have always favored as much immigration as would be politically feasible; this dynamic used to be popularly understood.

One person who understood the issue well was a black lesbian Democrat congresswoman from Houston. Barbara Jordan was the first African American elected to the Texas state senate since Reconstruction, and a staunch liberal and feminist. In 1994, Bill Clinton appointed her to be the chair of the U.S. Commission on Immigration Reform. The conclusions of the "Jordan Commission" sound like something you might hear Donald Trump use as talking points during a rally. Its report found that immigration most profoundly affects native-born high-school dropouts, accounting for 10 percent of the workforce, reducing their wages by around 5 percent. That may sound minor, but how would you like to make very little money and take a 5 percent pay cut? The Jordan Report[20] identified other costs that cause stress on local communities, including availability of housing, schools, hospitals, and recreation facilities.

The report suggested that the United States cut legal immigration by at least a third and eliminate "chain migration," which permits immigrants gradually to bring in dozens of relatives in the name of "family unification." Jordan suggested that immigration regulations should focus on admitting high-skilled applicants and eliminating the visa lottery; and, most important, structure our immigration policy to favor the country, not the immigrants who wish to come here. "We disagree with those who would label efforts to control immigration as being inherently anti-immigrant," explained the report. "Rather, it is both a right and a responsibility of a democratic society to manage immigration so that it serves the national interest."

Eugene McCarthy, the liberal Democratic senator from Minnesota who challenged Lyndon Johnson in 1968 for the presidential nomination (LBJ, of course, left the race, and vice-president Hubert Humphrey, also of Minnesota, was that year's nominee) wrote a curious book about immigration. *A Colony of the World: The United States Today*, published in 1992, offers the tendentious and somewhat quarrelsome thesis that America is in a "colonial relationship" vis-á-vis various domestic special interests, including big business, the legendary military-industrial complex, the foreign policy establishment, and so on.

But McCarthy specifies that one "mark of a country's colonial dependence is lack of control over its own borders, either as defined and mapped, with mother countries, international agencies or other outside authorities changing the lines, or abolishing them; or, if the lines are firm, lack of control over who or what crosses those borders."[21] This remark echoed Ronald Reagan, who is credited with having said, "A nation that cannot control its borders is not a nation," and predicted the candidacy of Donald Trump.[22]

It's incredible to consider the fact that "national interest" no longer has any place in the debate about immigration among the American Left. Talking about the interests of the nation in the context of immigration is derided as jingoistic, racist, and exclusionary, even among moderate Democrats. Immigrants, we are told constantly, do the jobs "that Americans won't do." But that argument overlooks that fact that Americans have always done—and still do—all sorts of jobs, including tedious, dirty, and difficult work like cleaning toilets, butchering animals, and picking crops. When people insist that immigrants do the jobs that Americans are too lazy and spoiled to do, what they mean is that Americans don't want to do those jobs for the same pay that desperate people from Third World countries are willing to accept.

Barbara Jordan's report insisted that the government must increase immigration enforcement on the border as well within the interior. It praised deportation as an important tool. "Credibility in immigration policy," it explained, "can be summed up in one sentence: those who should get in, get in; those who should be kept out, are kept out; and those who should not be here will be required to leave."

So, given all that, why does Donald Trump's promise to enforce existing immigration law, and to deport people who are here unlawfully, strike people as cruel, tyrannical, and racist?

The answer gets to a central redefinition of what it means to be an American that took place in the period after World War II. The dominant narrative of the American experience for its first 150 years or so was that the land had been settled by people seeking religious freedom, and the nation was founded by men so committed to the principle of political liberty that they were willing to die for it. The story of America post-founding was of the exploration and conquering of the Western frontier and the pacification of the Indians. The Civil War arose out of an intense disagreement about the nature of the original compact among the states and ended with the abolition of slavery, paid for with the deaths of 750,000 soldiers, or 1 out of every 40 people in the country.

Following World War II, key figures in the burgeoning civil rights movement sought to redefine the American story in a way that would reflect the changing demographics of the country. The American founders were Protestants of English descent, and the White majority of the nation reflected a mix of people from England and Scotland, Germany, and the Low Countries. European immigration continued through the nineteenth century, especially from Ireland, Germany, and Scandinavia; starting in the 1880s, a new wave of immigrants came from southern and eastern Europe, including millions of Italians, Slavs, and Jews. And, of course, America always had a significant number of blacks, descendants of the 600,000 African slaves who had been brought to North America over the course of almost 200 years.

Beginning in the early twentieth century, a new story of the American experience began to take hold, based less on the settlement of land and the conquering of the frontier, and more on the steady flow of immigrants who came to the United States to engage in the promise of the growing country. English author Israel Zangwill, so taken with the new American experiment in the intermingling of nations, was inspired to pen a drama about it called *The Melting Pot*.

This 1908 play, whose audience included President Theodore Roosevelt in attendance on its opening night, detailed the improbable story of a Jewish refugee from the notorious 1903 Kishinev massacre, in which his family had been slaughtered, who moves to America and composes a symphony in praise of a future world in which ethnic and sectarian differences have melted away. He falls in love with a beautiful Christian girl from Russia, who, as it happens, is the daughter of the very same officer who had ordered the massacre of the hero's family. All is forgiven, and the couple are betrothed as the curtain falls. President Roosevelt, so moved by the conclusion, shouted from his box, "That's a great play, Mr. Zangwill. A great play!"[23]

"America is God's Crucible," declares David Quixano, Zangwill's protagonist. "The great Melting-Pot where all the races of Europe are melting and re-forming! These are the fires of God you've come to—these are the fires of God. A fig for your feuds and vendettas! Germans and Frenchmen, Irishmen and Englishmen, Jews and Russians—into the Crucible with you all! God is making the American."

The language is florid and over the top, but the sentiment of America as a melting pot persists—or, at least, persisted—as the dominant narrative of the American experience, until the arrival of multiculturalism, and its rejection of assimilationism, beginning around the 1990s. A week before his 1976 election to the presidency, Jimmy Carter indicated this transition from the crucible ideal—whereby raw human material is amalgamated into a new human type—toward a vision of America as a "beautiful mosaic. Different people, different beliefs, different yearnings, different hopes, different dreams."[24]

But still today, we are nevertheless told, over and over, that America is, was, and always will be a "nation of immigrants," who either came here from somewhere else or are descended (excepting Native Americans) from someone who did. *A Nation of Immigrants* is, in fact, the title of a lesser-known 1958 pamphlet by then-senator and later president John F. Kennedy, and it appears to be a key source of the phrase. Sponsored by the Anti-Defamation League as part of its One Nation Library, the volume criticized the country's quota system for immigration, established in 1924, which based new admissions on each nationality's share of the total U.S. population according to the 1920 census. This system favored immigration from northern and western Europe and disfavored immigrants from Asia or Africa in particular. It is worth noting that immigration from Latin America was unrestricted and not subject to quotas.[25]

The Immigration Act of 1924 followed decades of a human influx to America's shores that was unprecedented in world history. By 1910, close to 15 percent of the American population had been born abroad, a level that was matched again only recently. The horrors of World War I, which took the lives of more than 117,000 soldiers in only 18 months, made many Americans think twice about the wisdom of foreign adventuring, and confirmed suspicions that the country would be better off attending to its own affairs. Political violence driven by hardcore anarchist terrorists, mostly from southern and eastern Europe, also made even sophisticated Americans wonder about the negative consequences of an open border policy.

The anti-immigrant sentiment that led to the 1924 Immigration Act has been called nativist, racist, antisemitic, and close-minded, and indeed, it did represent the high point of the influence of eugenic theory on national policy. Yet, proponents nevertheless suggested that the United States needed to take a "breathing spell" in immigration in order to absorb the millions of new Americans who had been taken in over the prior 40 years, and the population at large accepted the idea.

As president, Kennedy proposed scrapping the quota system, but he was murdered before any such legislation could advance. Following Kennedy's death, his successor, Lyndon Johnson, presided over the most significant expansion of federal civil rights legislation in a century, with the Civil Rights Acts of 1964 and the Voting Rights Act of 1965. But as important to the future of America, though passed and discussed with less fanfare, was the Immigration and Nationality Act of 1965. This measure radically opened up the strictures of the immigration reform of the 1920s, in particular allowing for significantly more migration from Asia.

Debate over the 1965 law in Congress raised some intriguing questions. Changing the national quota system for immigration was by no means driven by popular sentiment, which a Gallup Poll found to be against opening immigration to the world. Concerns that America would be swamped by Third World immigrants who would radically change the composition of the country were laughed off as absurd by supporters of the bill. "The bill will not flood our cities with immigrants," Senator Ted Kennedy said during debate. "It will not upset the ethnic mix of our society. It will not relax the standards of admission. It will not cause American workers to lose their jobs."[26]

Hiram Fong, senator from Hawaii, made similar predictions. "Asians represent six-tenths of 1 percent of the population of the United States . . . the people from that part of the world will never reach 1 percent of the population. . . . Our cultural pattern will never be changed as far as America is concerned."[27] Senator Claiborne Pell of Rhode Island was blunter, averring, "contrary to the opinions of some of the misinformed, this legislation does not open the floodgates."[28]

For good or ill, the Immigration and Nationality Act of 1965 *did* change the demographic and cultural pattern of the United States, significantly and undeniably. Throughout the first two-thirds of the twentieth century, the American population was roughly 90 percent white and 10 percent black. The Asian population was less than 1 percent. The Hispanic population was roughly 5 percent, and concentrated in the Southwest and California, where Mexican Americans had lived for many generations and whose presence was a known and understood quantity in the region.

Today, almost entirely as a function of legal immigration, America is a totally different country in terms of its racial and ethnic composition from how it was in 1965 or would have otherwise been. According to the Pew Research Center, immigrants and the birth of their children and grandchildren are responsible for 55 percent of the growth in the nation's population since 1965, which amounts to roughly 75 million people.[29] This astounding shift represents one of the largest movements of people across borders in world history. White non-Hispanics are now about 58 percent of the population, and that figure is shrinking fast. African Americans are about 12 percent of the population. About one in five Americans is Latino, of any race, and 6 percent are Asians. Mixed-race people are roughly 4 percent of the population.

It is possible to argue that the country was impoverished owing to its lack of diversity, and that it is now much better off because we now have a broader mix of people. But it is simply a fact that the Immigration and Nationality Act changed the country irrevocably and completely. This is a value-free judgment. I am not saying that it's bad or good. But you can't say it didn't happen.

Debate about the Immigration and Nationality Act directly connected its passage to the expansive civil rights legislation of the year before. Eliminating racism from American public life was explicitly cited as a basis for removing nation-based quotas from immigration law. Phillip Burton, a Democrat congressman from San Francisco, made this point when he spoke in favor of the Act, noting, "Just as we sought to eliminate discrimination in our land through the Civil Rights Act, today we seek by phasing out the national origins quota system to eliminate discrimination in immigration to this nation composed of the descendants of immigrants."[30]

Burton, an influential liberal whose seat and ideological orientation were later occupied by Nancy Pelosi, laid bare the real, though unstated, purpose of the 1965 Immigration Act, which was to establish an implicit right to immigrate to the United States that overrides executive or statutory authority. The idea of "discrimination in immigration" as a bad thing has come to dominate the way we think about immigration in America today, and it underwrites the reflexive hostility and accusations of racism that flare up whenever the topic of restricting immigration arises. Phillip Burton expressed the sentiment clearly: just as the owner of a restaurant has no right to restrict entry based on race, so the people of America have no right to decide who comes to settle here. America as such belongs as much to people who have never been here as it does to people born here.

Steve Sailer, a widely read and cited "noticer" of inconvenient facts, has called this sensibility the unwritten "Zeroth Amendment" to the Constitution, preceding and preempting all the others. Writing in December 2015, in response to a nonbinding "sense of the Senate" resolution that "the United States must not bar individuals from entering into the United States based on their religion, as such action would be contrary to the fundamental principles on which this Nation was founded," Sailer quipped that "the dominant ideological logic is trending toward making it inevitable that all 7 billion noncitizens on Earth be assumed to have civil rights to move to America."[31]

The theme that America is a "nation of immigrants" is used to justify a policy of unlimited immigration—or at least to obstruct any efforts to limit it. The implicit argument is that America, having been created by immigrants, owes it to future immigrants to continue the promise of the American Dream, virtually as a matter of debt. For example, in 2015, while running for the Democratic nomination for president, Hillary Clinton gave a major speech on immigration in which she proclaimed, "We are a country where people of all backgrounds, all nations of origin, all languages, all religions, all races, can make a home. America was built by immigrants."[32]

The idea that America "was built by immigrants" is appealing on its face, but some of its premises fall short. There is a clear distinction between "immigrants" on one hand and "colonists" or "settlers" on the other. The founders of the United States were not immigrants, because they came to a land that was largely undeveloped and that offered little or nothing in the way of public resources or infrastructure to newcomers.

And what does it even mean or matter that America was "built by immigrants," in terms of letting in more immigrants today? In 2012, Barack Obama's White House asked us to remember that "generations of immigrants have helped lay the railroads and build our cities, pioneer new industries and fuel our Information Age, from Google to the iPhone."[33] It is a common theme among commenters and politicians to praise the historical contribution of immigrants to America as a means of deflecting attention from the question as it relates to today. People who wish to migrate to America do not think of themselves as active participants in the narrative of the "nation of immigrants."

And the experience of immigrants who came to the United States in the great wave of nineteenth- and early-twentieth-century immigration is difficult to compare with any honesty to the expectations of immigrants who come today. In 1900, the United States had a population of 76 million people. About two in every five employed persons worked on farms.[34] Meanwhile, the country's manufacturing base was exploding; between 1900 and 1920, the number of people working in factories almost doubled.

In 1900, having little to no education was not a significant barrier to getting a job. Only about 6 percent of native-born

Americans had graduated from high school, and it was not considered precocious to leave school after eighth grade to join the workforce.[35] Child labor was still common in textile mills. Conditions were frequently brutal, with long hours, no job protection, no minimum wage, and horribly unsafe worksites. Immigrants who arrived in America with few skills or even knowledge of English could make their way throughout the country to work in agriculture, mines, mills, or garment factories or as domestic servants. America ran on muscle.

America in 1900, and for decades to follow, had no government-sponsored social safety net. There were no food stamps or unemployment insurance. There was no Medicaid—the health insurance for lower-income people that covers close to 100 million people in America today. There was no Supplemental Security Income benefits program, which today provides five million disabled people with monthly support. States and cities did not subsidize affordable housing; nor did they really regulate how housing was built or tenanted. There were no homeless shelters or a guaranteed "right to shelter," as exists in New York City. There were laws against vagrancy that could get you locked up if you were loitering without any money in your pocket.

The deal America offered immigrants was that they could come here and try to make a go of it, but if they were to fail, failure would hurt. Most immigrants in the great human wave around 1900 were no less skilled than their American counterparts, but the levels of skill demanded back then to make it in the economy were much lower than they are today. A lot of immigrants decided to go home after trying their luck here. Millions of Italians came to America, especially in the first decade of the twentieth century, but roughly 40 percent went back to Italy after five years.[36]

America today is a vastly different country from how it was during the previous high-water mark of immigration 125 years ago. Today, only about 2 percent of the workforce is employed in agriculture. Our nation has shifted from one in which muscle has primacy to a service-based economy. The country's largest employment sectors are professional and business services, healthcare and social assistance, and government work. Our economy demands training and education for people to succeed and get ahead, and both legal and illegal immigrants tend to have lower levels of education and, of course, English proficiency than native-born citizens.

Advocates for immigrants today skip over a lot of this history in favor of drawing a straight line of sentimental balderdash between the past and the present. Suggestions that America adopt a skills-based framework for accepting immigrants, as Canada and Australia once did, which would consider the human resource needs of the United States rather than the desires of the potential immigrants, are routinely disparaged as racist. Moreover, advocates, to a comically predictable degree, frequently make a special appeal based on their own family history.

For example, in 2017 when the Trump administration proposed assessing English competency and professional skills as grounds for legal admission, New York City mayor Bill de Blasio derided the idea because it would have, retrospectively, barred his grandmother from entry. As a reporter covering the mayor at the time, I asked him, "You seem to say that we shouldn't have tests for proficiency of English or skilled workers. They say there's about a billion people in the world who would like to come to the United States. What kind of criteria do you think are appropriate for the country to decide who comes in, or is it really not up to the United States, and it's just a matter of what the people who want to come think?"

De Blasio's response was illuminating:

What President Trump proposed literally would have excluded my grandparents, and probably would have excluded the parents and grandparents of a lot of the people in this room. My grandparents didn't speak English when they got here from Italy. My grandparents didn't have college degrees. They became exemplary Americans. Their children were able to go to college . . . that's the American dream. The notion that we only want to admit people who speak English and have advanced degrees violates the history of almost 400 years of people coming here, including working-class people, folks who didn't have education, folks who didn't have the benefit of knowing English—and yet, they built this country.[37]

Your author, being something of a wag, pointed out to de Blasio that, had his grandmother not been admitted to the United States, New York City would still have a mayor today, anyway.

David J. Skorton, the former president of Cornell University, writing in *USA Today* on Independence Day 2018 in his capacity as the head of the Smithsonian Institution, made a similarly special plea for future immigrants based on the history of his own family. "One hundred years ago," he began, "my father and his family emigrated from Russia to start a new life in the U.S." After running through the familiar litany of successful immigrants and their many achievements, Skorton concluded by noting, "In our present difficult moment, it's important to reflect on our history and remember how much America has benefited by choosing to embrace, rather than exclude, immigrants from a diverse range of backgrounds."

According to de Blasio's and Skorton's perspective, the reason why America must never change its immigration laws is because, had the laws been different 120 years ago, the country would never have had the benefit of . . . themselves! This idiotic argument—"Imagine a world without me"—is quite common, especially among highly educated people who take it for granted that their existence is manifestly a common good for everyone else.

This position would readily be called insane if applied to any other matter of public policy. In a rational society, matters such as immigration would be treated the same way that traffic control measures or agricultural subsidies are dealt with. The various interested parties could make their voices heard, and legislators could set policy accordingly. But in the domain of immigration, consideration of all economic, national, political, and sociological effects is suspended in favor of people who have never entered the country, and their desire to have "a better life."

The "better life" argument, more than anything else, shifts the debate about immigration away from the interests of Americans and prioritizes the desires of the potential migrants. Nancy Pelosi frequently cited the better life that migrants sought as justification for their presence here. In June 2021, serving as speaker of the House, Pelosi tweeted, "During National Immigrant Heritage Month, we honor those who came to the United States to build a better life. There is nothing more American than the hope & courage that immigrant communities display every day. #CelebrateImmigrants."[38]

If you have never heard of or celebrated National Immigrant Heritage Month, I am positive you are not alone. But it makes you wonder why we need to "honor those who came to the United States to build a better life." Wanting to move to a nicer place with more economic opportunity and better schools and healthcare may be understandable . . . but *honorable*? Wanting a "better life" for yourself or your family is normal, but it hardly implies that you are a noble or moral person. José Inez García Zárate, presumably, was seeking a better life for himself when he entered the United States illegally for the fourth or fifth time to pursue his career manufacturing and selling small-batch methamphetamine, and his hobby of aimlessly shooting at sea lions in San Francisco Bay.

But even if someone wants to come here legally to open a perfectly legal business or work in a respectable field to make a better life for himself and his family . . . so what? No one will explain why the simple desire to improve one's standing in life by moving to the United States is a net positive for the people who are already here, and the entire debate about immigration seems to be structured to foreclose the possibility of asking that question.

This book isn't about immigration, pro or con. There are plenty of such books, and there are plenty of arguments in favor of and against immigration, both legal and illegal. But the country does have a set of laws regarding the proper way to enter America, who can work here, and the rules regarding deportation. Why is enforcement of the law such a political third rail?

Donald Trump's plan to build a wall between Mexico and the United States evoked a kind of seething disgust and horror akin to a formal suggestion that the federal government ought to reinstitute the African slave trade. Mention of the wall became an externalization of how Trump's opponents viewed his supporters: dumb, blank, and obstructive.

It was commonly observed in the media that, though walls may seem like a good way to keep people out of a given area, in fact they are useless and counterproductive. *Rolling Stone* ran a characteristic example of the genre in 2019 called "Six Historians on Why Trump's Border Wall Won't Work." According to the experts consulted by *Rolling Stone*, who cited the Maginot Line and the Berlin Wall as negative examples, "border walls have failed time and again throughout history. . . . So, why have governments continued to fall back on the idea of erecting such physical barriers?"[39]

It could be pointed out that walls may eventually fail, but they usually do a pretty good job up to the point of failure of preserving the integrity of a given space. The Maginot Line, which was France's line of defense against German invasion before World War II, famously failed only because it wasn't long enough—the invading German army just went around it. And the Berlin Wall worked astoundingly well at keeping East Germans from defecting en masse to the West. It worked fine, as a wall; it only fell when the regime maintaining it collapsed.

If walls didn't work, they wouldn't be the oldest barrier technology known to humanity. Walls obviously work, which is why there was so much consternation about the idea of building one on the Mexican border. If the wall wouldn't have worked, who would care if they built it or not?

There are border walls all around the world, and while they may not keep everyone out, in general they do a pretty good job at keeping most people on the other side. Hungary erected a fence on its border to keep out migrants during the Syrian refugee crisis, and it immediately cut the number of illegal crossers by 99 percent. Israel maintains a security barrier between itself and the West Bank that has radically reduced the number of cross-border suicide bombings since the erection of the wall. If Israel had built a similarly strong wall on its border with Gaza, instead of a largely unguarded fence, Hamas would not have been able to break through it and perpetrate its massacre on October 7, 2023. The Demilitarized Zone between North Korea and South Korea is virtually impermeable. Greece and Turkey; Poland and Belarus; Spain and Morocco; Haiti and the Dominican Republic—all of these neighboring countries and more have or are building physical barriers to prevent illegal immigration or smuggling.

The most impassioned arguments against Trump's wall draw a poetic contrast between architectonic forms. "We need to build bridges, not walls," said Hillary Clinton. "Instead of building walls, we can help build bridges," intoned Mark Zuckerberg. "A person who thinks only about building walls, wherever they may be, and not building bridges, is not Christian," said Pope Francis, who lived within a walled city-state. "Life is best when you build bridges between people, not walls," said Billy Crystal (at Muhammad Ali's funeral). The former president of Mexico, the Canadian trade minister, Kim Kardashian—everyone agrees that it is better to build bridges, which *join* people, instead of walls, which *divide* people.

While the "bridges/walls" theme has a certain campfire resonance of brotherly togetherness, its advocates seem to forget that they are speaking metaphorically about bridges. Trump promised to build a real wall. While a real bridge might pose a separate and contradictory purpose to a real wall, imaginary bridges and actual walls could coexist and serve complementary functions.

Immigration enthusiasts have long pointed silently to Emma Lazarus's 1883 poem "The New Colossus," which was added to the base of the Statue of Liberty in 1903, as the final word in their argument; wall opponents have made Robert Frost's "Mending Wall" their prooftext. "As Robert Frost reminds us: 'Something there is that doesn't love a wall,'" writes Brookings Institution senior fellow Vanda Felbab-Brown. Something there may be, though the same poem states the opposing sentiment—"Good fences make good neighbors." The speaker of that line is the narrator's neighbor, who emerges from darkness, "a stone grasped firmly by the top/In each hand, like an old-stone savage armed." Frost's poem is steeped in ambiguity about the purpose of fences. Its very meaning balances precariously atop the titular wall, like one of the rocks that the narrator places and prays to remain where he put it. Poets may be, in Shelley's words, the unacknowledged legislators of the world; but the fact that they are unacknowledged is precisely the reason why we don't apply their words literally.[40]

In 1987, Ronald Reagan issued one of the most quoteworthy presidential statements of the twentieth century when he commanded then-Soviet leader Mikhail Gorbachev to tear down the Berlin Wall. Taken by true believers as prophetic, Reagan's words are held out as an example of how degraded Trump's vision was, compared with that of the man whose shoes he tried to fill. *The New Yorker*'s John Lee Anderson savors the irony of Trump, "boisterously claiming he wants to build a new [wall], not to keep out Communists, or even the ISIS terrorists he mysteriously claims to know how to eliminate, but people from Mexico, our closest neighbor to the south, a friendly nation." Doug Elmets, a former Reagan speechwriter, spoke at the 2016 Democratic National Convention. "Reagan famously said, 'Tear down this wall,'" Elmets said. "Trump says, 'Build the wall.'"[41]

The Berlin Wall was a prison designed to keep people *in*. A wall on the U.S.–Mexican border would keep people *out*. That difference is as significant as the difference between capitalist democracy and a Communist dictatorship, or between lawlessness and the rule of law.

Immediately upon the election of Joe Biden to the White House, an unprecedented surge of migrants flooded the U.S. border. Raul Ortiz, Biden's appointed head of the U.S. Border Patrol, conceded in a 2022 deposition that migrants apprehended at the border had heard from social media that the new policies of the Biden administration had made it much easier to cross and get released into the United States.

Coached in the international language of human rights law, hundreds of thousands of migrants intoned the magic words, "I have a well-founded fear of persecution," which, according to the Biden administration's loose interpretation of asylum law, granted them immediate admission to the country, with a court hearing scheduled years in the future. Would they be allowed to stay here forever? Maybe not—most asylum claims are ultimately rejected. But in the meantime, the applicants would be allowed to live and usually work here, travel freely, set down roots and community ties, and have children. And if they were to fail to show up for check-ins or court . . . well, they could just join the other millions of "undocumented" immigrants.

Prior to the 2022 midterm election, Florida governor Ron DeSantis, Texas governor Greg Abbott, and Arizona governor Doug Ducey decided dramatically to spotlight the border crisis by chartering buses and planes to send migrants to New York City; Washington, D.C.; Martha's Vineyard; and other Democrat strongholds. The Biden administration had studiously been ignoring the fact that close to 10,000 people a day were flooding the border, and the national media were essentially not reporting the story at all, because it could have adversely affected the Democrats' electoral efforts. The Republican governors organized their stunt to force attention on this key issue.

The media responded predictably, huffing in outrage about what they called an exploitative and possibly illegal form of human trafficking. Television ran puff pieces about the heroic humanitarian efforts of the residents of tony resort island Martha's Vineyard—where Barack Obama has a 30-acre vacation estate— who immediately organized transport for the needy migrants . . . back to the mainland.

In New York, local politicians and advocates who have long trumpeted the high moral ground of the nation's sanctuary city *par excellence* demanded federal intervention to manage the influx of a few dozen migrants. "It's clear that Governor Abbott is attempting to make this into a political prop using people who are seeking to live the American dream as the prop for him," said New York

City's then-mayor Eric Adams, "and it's just really unfortunate. It's inhumane, it's un-American and it's unethical." Lori Lightfoot, then the mayor of Chicago, called Abbott's measures "racist."[42]

The red state governors organized transport north for about 10,000 migrants over the course of six months, roughly the same number who crossed the border into Texas every day. But while leftist pols and their friends in the media complained bitterly about this supposedly unprecedented human rights violation that would stress local sanctuary cities, punishing them for their generosity, the federal government has been engaging in similar practices for decades. Migrants who cross the border and make a claim for asylum are routinely released to await a court hearing, which can take up to seven years. In the meantime, they are offered transit and steered to jurisdictions around the country where politically connected aid groups assist them in taking advantage of the generosity of local communities.

Tens of thousands of Somalis were settled in the United States following the East African nation's vicious civil war, and the country's largest Somali community is in Minnesota. Media reports about the unlikely presence of people from equatorial Africa in America's northern heartland usually focus on the human-interest aspect—first snowfall, sampling "hotdish," teaching the locals about Islam—but the real origin story of Somalis in Minnesota involves refugee resettlement groups called VOLAGs ("voluntary agencies"). VOLAGs contract with the federal government to settle refugees, and then hunt around for likely spots to place them.

"There is so much goodness in this state," said Somali-born Ahmed Samatar, dean of the Institute for Global Citizenship at Macalester College, in a 2011 interview with CBS News, explaining why his compatriots, after being settled in Minnesota by Lutheran Social Services and Catholic Charities, elected to stay. The "goodness" he referenced means the extensive welfare and generous services that Minnesota offers its needy. "The institutions of this state, private or public, have an important place in the mind of Somalis," said Samatar, explaining why so many waves of Somali migrants have followed their fellows to the Land of 10,000 Lakes. "Minnesota is exceptional in so many ways, but it's the closest thing in the United States to a true social democratic state," Samatar observed.

The largesse of Minnesota's experiment in social democracy was amply demonstrated in 2018, when Customs and Border Protection officers at Minneapolis-St. Paul Airport noted that certain travelers en route to Somalia were regularly leaving the country with suitcases filled with up to one million dollars in U.S. currency. It is legal to transport such sums as long as they are declared, but investigations soon revealed that the individuals carrying the money were tied to a massive fraud, possibly amounting to $100 million annually. Minnesota's Child Care Assistance Program (CCAP), it emerged, had been reimbursing bogus daycares, all run by Somali migrants, for millions of dollars for care that was never provided. The sums involved amounted to one-third of the state's entire CCAP budget; much of it is suspected to have wound up financing the actions of al-Shabaab, the Somali al-Qaeda affiliate.

It's no surprise that migrants to a rich, credulous country would try to take advantage of free money; even Americans who have been here for ten generations have been known to bilk the system, after all. Yet, in the "Fool me once, shame on you; fool me twice, shame on me" category, Minnesota's social democratic social services infrastructure seems more willing than most to be fooled over and over again. In 2022, then-Attorney General Merrick Garland announced charges against four dozen Minnesotans—almost all of them Somali migrants—for carrying out the nation's largest Covid-19 fraud scheme.[43]

The fraud, amounting to $250 million, centered on a federally funded meal program administered by the state of Minnesota by a group called Feeding our Future. The people behind Feeding Our Future "opened more than 250 sites throughout the state of Minnesota and fraudulently obtained and disbursed more than $240 million in Federal Child Nutrition Program funds. The defendants used the proceeds of their fraudulent scheme to purchase luxury vehicles, residential and commercial real estate in Minnesota as well as property in Ohio and Kentucky, real estate in Kenya and Turkey, and to fund international travel," according to the Department of Justice.

Every society has rent-seeking individuals who try to work the system. Immigrant communities in a rich country like the United States always have members who exploit the host people's sense of generosity, as well as the naivete of the greenhorns who have just arrived from their home countries. It's not fair to adduce some bad examples as probative of the negative impact of immigration, just as it doesn't make much sense to suggest that Google founder Sergey Brin, born in the Soviet Union and brought here as a child, is a representative immigrant—though he is so cited all the time.

What is interesting about this case in particular is how readily social service functionaries in the Gopher State were willing to collaborate with federally funded VOLAGs to assist Somali scammers in fleecing the people of Minnesota, repeatedly. State employees evidently pointed out to the operators of bogus daycares that they were eligible for reimbursement for the meals they provided to their imaginary wards, and helped them fill out the paperwork to collect the additional funds.

Curiously enough, a federal law making it easier for people to send money abroad was sponsored by then-Congressman Keith Ellison, the first Muslim elected to Congress. Now the attorney general of Minnesota, Ellison was succeeded in his Somali-heavy district by Somali native Ilhan Omar. Ellison made the facilitation of remittances from America to Somalia by his constituents a key policy priority of his term in office. He introduced the bill that became the Money Remittances Improvement Act of 2014. This law, which was passed by voice vote in the House and Senate, relaxed federal oversight over international money transfers, making it possible for loosely regulated "money service businesses," such as check-cashing storefronts, to send money overseas. "Passage of the Money Remittances Improvement Act is cause for celebration for all diaspora communities, including the Somali and Hmong communities I am proud to represent in Minnesota," Ellison said at the time.[44]

In October 2015, Minnesota's then-governor Mark Dayton, whose family founded Target, made an illuminating comment regarding the need for more immigration from Somalia and other places. "Our economy cannot expand based on white, B+, Minnesota-born citizens," explained Dayton, in a St. Cloud forum. "We don't have enough."[45]

It may sound odd for a governor to disparage the existing population of his state as inadequate to the task of keeping the richest state in the Midwest prosperous. After all, it was largely native-born Minnesotans who built the state in the first place, and it is certainly they who pay the taxes that allow the only social democracy in America to offer the generous benefits that lure valuable non-white, grade A+, non-native-born Minnesotans to move there.

The response to Dayton's remarks about the benefits of immigration provides an intriguing contrast to those of Donald Trump about the same topic a few months earlier. Trump disparaged the quality of illegal immigrants, saying that Mexico wasn't "sending their best." Dayton disparaged the quality of the existing population of Minnesota, characterizing them as "B+"—okay, but not top-notch. (Given native-born Minnesotan Garrison Keillor's famous joke about his fictional town of Lake Wobegon, "where all the children are above average," we can assume that "B+" does not indicate high praise.)

In any case, Trump brought down the wrath of the educated classes and elite media for suggesting that people who seek illegal entry into a neighboring country might not represent the cream of their own society; and nobody except a few conservative bloggers took note of Dayton saying that his own constituents were basically a bunch of mediocrities in need of immediate supplementation if not outright replacement.

"Replacement theory" is the hypothesis that mass immigration from the Third World is, at best, a plan to flood the country with future Democrat voters or, more diabolically, a plot to end white supremacy by reducing the white American majority to a minority. Originally formulated by novelist and gay liberationist -turned-anti-migration activist Renaud Camus to describe the mass importation of North African Muslims into France as orchestrated by a "replacist" elite to eliminate the native European white population, it was quickly noticed by observers in Germany, Britain, and other countries to be taking place there, too.

Replacement theory earned a spectacularly bad name in America during the 2017 "Unite the Right" rally in Charlottesville, Virginia, when some unsavory white nationalist types marched with tiki torches chanting either "You will not replace us," or "Jews will not replace us," or maybe both. This was the same weekend that a white nationalist plowed a car into a crowd, killing a protester; when Trump was alleged to praise Nazis as "fine people" (he did not, as a simple reading of remarks reveals); and that Joe Biden cited as his inspiration for entering the 2020 race.

The replacement hypothesis was thus thrust into the national discourse and explained everywhere as a demented, racist conspiracy theory that is not just wrong, a hoax, and a myth, but extremely dangerous. NPR quotes Adolphus Belk Jr., professor of political science and African American studies at Winthrop University, explaining how replacement theory proponents fear that "whites will no longer be a majority of the general population, but a plurality, and see that as a threat to their own well-being and the well-being of the nation."[46] People who accept replacement theory, says Belk, "are willing to use any means that are available to preserve and defend their position in society . . . it's almost like a sort of holy war, a conflict, where they see themselves as taking the action directly to the offending culture and people by eliminating them."

Many organizations have identified replacement theory as heinous and beyond the limits of acceptable discourse. The Anti-Defamation League and the Southern Poverty Law Center both fundraise off the threat that replacement theory poses. To be fair, a number of murderers, including the lunatic who killed ten black people at a Buffalo grocery store, have cited replacement theory as a motive for their actions, and it's certainly true that the hypothesis can easily fit snugly with certain paranoid worldviews.

And yet, it's intriguing to flip the argument of replacement theory around and look at it from another side. There is a history dating back decades of talking about inexorable demographic change in America, change that will slowly "brown" the country, turning average pigmentation darker, making the nation gradually less white, and irrevocably changing the demographics of the United States forever. This change, it is said explicitly and even happily, will reduce the power of the legacy white population of America, making the country different in many unpredictable ways, but certainly better. As the Brookings Institution, the Center for American Progress, and the American Enterprise Institute explained in a major 2016 report:

While shifting demographics favor Democrats when all
else is held equal, the party has significant vulnerability
among aging white voters. . . . On the other hand,
Republicans face a clear need to enhance their appeal to
America's rapidly growing minority population—especially
the new minorities of Hispanics and Asians. If they do
not, Republicans risk putting themselves into a box where
they become ever more dependent on a declining white
population—particularly its older segment.

In 2018, right before the midterm election, *New York Times*
columnist Michelle Goldberg penned an op-ed titled "We Can
Replace Them." In the article, Goldberg celebrates the upcoming
victory of Georgia's Stacey Abrams as the first black female governor in American history. (She lost, as it emerged.) Her opponent,
Brian Kemp, is the "candidate of aggrieved whiteness," the candidate of "an embittered white conservative minority [that] clings
to power, terrified at being swamped by a new multiracial poly-
glot majority." Reminding her reader that "Georgia is less than 53
percent non-Hispanic white," Goldberg concludes by telling voters to "do to white nationalists what they fear most. Show them
they're being replaced."[47]

One could argue that Goldberg is responding to the paranoia
around replacement rather than instigating it . . . but what's the
difference, especially when she throws the language of racial displacement directly into the argument? But we hardly have to rely
on Michelle Goldberg to find eager celebration of the decline of the
white population of the United States, and the anticipated surge in
the power of the nonwhite electorate. It's virtually everywhere.

In 2021, Republican-controlled state legislatures passed
laws concerning election security, which Democrats denounced
as efforts to suppress the vote. Illinois Democrat Senator Dick

Durbin explained his view of the Republicans' motives simply as a matter of their trying to keep their numbers up while "the demographics of America are not on the side of the Republican Party. The new voters in this country are moving away from them, away from Donald Trump, away from their party creed that they preach." In other words, immigration is changing the complexion of the electorate in a way that Democrats find favorable. Sounds a lot like replacement theory.[48]

In 2015, then Vice President Biden made some remarks at a White House event about terrorism and extremism. He related a conversation he had about America with Lee Kuan Yew, the first prime minister of Singapore. Biden said he told Yew that the key to America's success was "an unrelenting stream of immigration, nonstop, nonstop." Biden explained that "Folks like me who are Caucasian, of European descent, for the first time in 2017, we'll be in an absolute minority in the United States of America, absolute minority. Fewer than 50 percent of the people in America from then and on will be white European stock. That's not a bad thing, that's a source of our strength."[49]

Biden's estimate of 2017 as the point at which America will be "majority-minority" is about 30 years early, but his point that the decline of "white European stock" is a good thing is clear. He echoed these remarks in 2020 during his presidential race, tweeting, "Our diversity is, and has always been, our greatest strength as a nation."

This perspective is articulated by the other side, too, sometimes as vociferously or even more so. After Trump's 2024 election, his team began making plans for the rapid rollout of its agenda, and a divide quickly emerged between two factions of the "MAGA" camp. One side, identified with, if not strictly represented by, Steve Bannon and the America First contingent, advocated for a complete shutdown of immigration, both at the border and through special visa programs, especially H-1B visas. The other side, most prominently spoken for by former presidential candidate, tech bro millionaire, and "DOGE" efficiency expert Vivek Ramaswamy, offered a different point of view.

H-1B visas were invented in the early nineties in order to let "highly skilled" foreigners work in the United States on a non-immigrant basis, supposedly to alleviate a shortage of American workers in tech fields. According to federal guidelines, these visas must not "adversely affect the wages and working conditions" of American workers, and employers who seek to hire foreign workers under H-1B provisions are, in theory, supposed to demonstrate that they have tried to hire American citizens and that they aren't just trying to undercut the wages of the upper-middle class.

Critics of the program insist that's exactly what H-1B visas do, in both effect and design. They call the program a massive, nefarious scam that large corporations use to import a cheap, pliable workforce. They point out that the system has been gamed to the point that 75 percent of H-1B visa recipients come from one country—India—and that they do, in fact, accept lower pay than the "prevailing wage" for such work. They say that American companies pour millions of dollars into lobbying for the expansion of the program, use it to hire platoons of foreign workers to come to the United States, and then force American workers to train their replacements, before firing them.[50]

During a Republican primary debate in 2016, candidate Donald Trump was asked about H-1B visas, and replied, "We shouldn't have it. Very, very bad for workers." Ronil Hira, author of *Outsourcing America*, testified to Congress in 2015 about the H-1B visa program:

> Congress and multiple Administrations have inadvertently
> created a highly lucrative business model of bringing

in cheaper H-1B workers to substitute for Americans. There are mainframe-sized loopholes built into the H-1B program's design—the statutory law, regulations, administrative law, and policy guidance—and a complete disinterest on the part of multiple Administrations in enforcing the current rules, however weak they may be. Some of these loopholes are intentional, some are not, but they all add up to a system that encourages employers to exploit the H-1B program for cheap labor.[51]

The biggest tech companies in America routinely are the biggest applicants for H-1B visas. Alphabet (Google), Meta, Apple, Infosys, Microsoft, Salesforce—these corporations and others in their sector bring in tens of thousands of foreign workers, citing a "lack of talent" among the American workforce. Meanwhile, these same companies have been firing employees or offering severance packages to induce them to quit. Alphabet laid off 12,000 employees in January 2023, Meta fired 5 percent of its workforce in 2025, and Microsoft is "going harder" on layoffs, offering no severance to terminated workers.

Moreover, the H-1B program, while meant to provide employers with a temporary means of filling vacancies with foreign workers who are expected to go home within a few years, has become a back door for people seeking to move to the United States permanently. Immigration law firms specializing in "adjustment of status" advertise vigorously in H-1B-rich states like California and Texas, and Indian message boards are filled with advice on the best ways to manipulate the system.

Vivek Ramaswamy, whose 2024 campaign for president pledged "America First" and a promise to "revive American national identity," in early 2025 posted on X a defense of the H-1B

visa regime that many MAGA supporters read as a stark betrayal
of the movement:

- The reason top tech companies often hire foreign-born &
  first-generation engineers over "native" Americans isn't because
  of an innate American IQ deficit (a lazy & wrong explanation).
- A key part of it comes down to the c-word: culture. Tough
  questions demand tough answers & if we're really serious
  about fixing the problem, we have to confront the TRUTH:
  Our American culture has venerated mediocrity over excellence for way too long (at least since the 90s and likely longer).
- That doesn't start in college, it starts YOUNG. A culture
  that celebrates the prom queen over the math olympiad
  champ, or the jock over the valedictorian, will not produce
  the best engineers.
- A culture that venerates Cory from "Boy Meets World," or
  Zach & Slater over Screech in "Saved by the Bell," or 'Stefan'
  over Steve Urkel in "Family Matters," will not produce the
  best engineers.
- (Fact: I know *multiple* sets of immigrant parents in the
  90s who actively limited how much their kids could watch
  those TV shows precisely because they promoted mediocrity
  . . . and their kids went on to become wildly successful STEM
  graduates).
- More movies like Whiplash, fewer reruns of "Friends." More
  math tutoring, fewer sleepovers. More weekend science com-
  petitions, fewer Saturday morning cartoons. More books,
  less TV. More creating, less "chillin."
- More extracurriculars, less "hanging out at the mall." Most
  normal American parents look skeptically at "those kinds
  of parents."

- More normal American kids view such "those kinds of kids" with scorn. If you grow up aspiring to normalcy, normalcy is what you will achieve.
- Now close your eyes & visualize which families you knew in the 90s (or even now) who raise their kids according to one model versus the other. Be brutally honest. "Normalcy" doesn't cut it in a hyper-competitive global market for technical talent. And if we pretend like it does, we'll have our asses handed to us by China.
- This can be our Sputnik moment. We've awaken from slumber before & we can do it again. Trump's election hopefully marks the beginning of a new golden era in America, but only if our culture fully wakes up. A culture that once again prioritizes achievement over normalcy; excellence over mediocrity; nerdiness over conformity; hard work over laziness.[52]

Ramaswamy's comments, in the context of the H-1B debate, came off as out-of-touch and tone-deaf—fewer "Friends" reruns? No sleepovers?—but also as absurdly condescending. It's wonderful that he didn't say that Asian people have higher IQs than the average American, but his scorn for what he called American "culture"—hanging out at the mall and worshiping the prom queen—suggested that the United States had better change itself fast. And importing more Indians is the best way to do it.

The H-1B debate is funny, because it represents a weaponization of the idea of merit. Americans like meritocratic systems because they are democratic and reward people on an individual basis, based on their talent and hard work. So, the idea of orienting the American immigration system around merit sounds like it dovetails with how we approach life anyway. Canada and Australia have (or had) "points" systems to admit immigrants based on what they can add to those countries, and it's certainly a more rational system than just letting in anyone who shows up at the border, and then their families a few years down the road.

Vivek Ramaswamy, and to a lesser extent Elon Musk and Donald Trump, have spoken in favor of merit-based immigration. And Ramaswamy's odd tirade about sleepovers—like a lot of the rhetoric around H-1B visas—implies that Americans are soft and lazy and unwilling to pit themselves against the world's best. Moreover, proponents of merit-based immigration say, if America doesn't bring in the brightest computer programmers today from India, China, or parts unknown, we will have to compete against them tomorrow.

But where is it written that part of the American mission is to subject our children to ruthless competition in a Hunger Games–style battle royale?

The Preamble to the Constitution explicitly says that the purpose of forming the United States is to "secure the Blessings of Liberty to ourselves and our Posterity," that is, our descendants. It's not the job of Americans to submit themselves to some deranged principle of limitless competition derived from a misreading of the idea of free markets.

Writing in the 1950s, East German dramatist Bertolt Brecht responded to a Communist functionary's assertion that the people had squandered the confidence of the government and needed to work harder in order to win it back. "Would it not be simpler," Brecht wrote, "for the government to dissolve the people and elect another?" This droll comment expresses Ramaswamy's elitist annoyance that the American people have failed to reproduce themselves according to a tech oligarch's vision of an ideal worker. Let's get some new Americans in here, ASAP!

Let's stipulate that "diversity is America's strength," though it's not clear why this statement is necessarily true. The American motto, *E pluribus unum*, means exactly the opposite—that out of

many, we find unity as one people. It was because our early con-
federation was so "diverse," with 13 radically different states pursuing their individual interests, that it was weak and unworkable.
By subordinating themselves to the principle of being "united
states," they suppressed their diversity and became powerful.
Like teamwork.

But in what possible sense is diversity "our *greatest* strength"?
This sounds like one of those slogans out of George Orwell's
1984—"war is peace," "freedom is slavery"—the purpose of which
is to derail logic and substitute compliance for thought. Human
diversity is just a given because all people are different. But the
cult of diversity as a great strength only refers to *racial* diversity
and implies that people as people are basically the same, and real
human greatness can only be achieved by having more and more
people of different races. It's actually a profoundly inhuman perspective on life, because it obviates individuality in favor of general characteristics that have nothing to do with a person's innate
qualities or personal achievement.

The funny thing about replacement theory is that, depending
on who's talking about it, it is either a horrible thing to talk about,
or a cause for joy. Writer and former Trump White House official
Michael Anton calls this phenomenon the "Celebration Parallax,"
meaning that "the same fact pattern is either true and glorious or
false and scurrilous depending on who states it."[53]

Immigration occupies such a sensitive place in American
politics for a variety of reasons. It is widely understood among
the donor class, the bondholders, and the editorial writers of
America that immigration is an effective means to hold wages
down—from workplaces as varied as lettuce farms and meatpack-
ing plants to hospital emergency rooms and web 3.0 companies.

But immigration is a touchstone of deplorability, and opposing limits to it is an open statement of allegiance to a cosmopolitan

sensibility that sees America as a convenient place to hang one's hat, file lawsuits in the nation's robust and open legal system, invest money in America's open and transparent capital markets, and hire cheap workers in the name of letting them pursue their American Dream. The "better life" that immigrants seek may in fact become real for them. The problem is when their pursuit of a better life makes things worse for everyone else.

TWO

PUBLIC SAFETY

All Causes Are One Cause

Barack Obama ran for president in 2008 on the implicit promise that he, owing to his mixed-race parentage and political savvy, was uniquely capable of moving the country beyond its tortured racial past. He would unite the nation—black, white, and everything else—and push it toward a postracial future, as even his detractors hoped was possible.

In his 2004 keynote address at the Democratic National Convention, which he delivered before he was even elected to the U.S. Senate, Obama electrified the crowd and the nation with his stirring words of unity. "There's not a liberal America and a conservative America—there's the United States of America," he proclaimed. "There's not a black America and white America and Latino America and Asian America; there's the United States of America."[1]

Running for the Democratic nomination for president four years later, Obama again spoke expansively about race and the need to overcome the "old racial wounds" of the past. Obama addressed news reports about his former pastor and mentor Jeremiah Wright, who had thundered, "God damn America!" from the pulpit and, on the Sunday after 9/11, gloated that "America's chickens are coming home to roost." Acknowledging that Wright's comments were "divisive," Obama nevertheless insisted that it would be a mistake to "dismiss Reverend Wright as a crank or a demagogue." Obama explained that "black anger" and "white resentments" have created a "racial stalemate." But he concluded that the struggles and aspirations of Americans of all races could unite us in our quest for "a more perfect union."[2]

The reaction to Obama's speech among Democrats and the mainstream media was enthusiastic. NBC News said it was the best political speech of the decade. George Stephanopoulos, a product of the Bill Clinton White House, spoke on ABC News of Obama's "remarkable speech about race and his own journey, and his relationship with Wright in Philadelphia. That held his campaign together; a very key moment."

Though Obama's speech received plaudits and is credited with salvaging a campaign that was on the verge of cratering, a careful reading of the address reveals that its tone of conciliation and path-building disguises a deeper message of conflict and division. The speech opened by reflecting that the Constitution—which was written across the street from where Obama was speaking—"was stained by this nation's original sin of slavery." This stain, he maintained, required "protests and struggle, on the streets and in the courts, through a civil war and civil disobedience and always at great risk" to close the "gap between the promise of our ideals and the reality of their time."

Talking about slavery as America's "original sin" is certainly common, and it's a handy expression that everyone can nod along to. But original sin has a very specific theological meaning, and the implications of the term are weighted. "Original Sin," in the technical sense, is a Christian—not Abrahamic, because Jews and Muslims reject it—understanding of the Fall of Man in Genesis, the first chapter of the Bible. The meaning of Original Sin in this sense is that, because Adam and Eve disobeyed God, all of humanity is burdened or stained by their actions. We are all born depraved. And the only way out of this trap is through divine intercession—either the grace of God, or accepting Jesus, or whatever other method Christian theology has devised.

Leftists wouldn't be comfortable comparing abortion to Herod's Massacre of the Innocents, nor would they accept a parallel between the destruction of Sodom and Gomorrah and AIDS. They wouldn't be happy about calling a woman wearing lipstick Jezebel and having her eaten by dogs. Leftists frequently demand that Christian moralism and matters of state be kept separate, yet they casually talk about slavery in hamartiological—the theology of sin—terms all the time.

This is a problem because, if chattel slavery is America's original sin, then there is no worldly, normal way to fix it. Banning the importation of slaves, as Congress did in 1808, won't do it. Fighting a civil war that kills or maims over a million people (3 percent of the country's population) won't do it. Amending the Constitution won't do it. Judicial and legislative civil rights measures won't do it. The creation of a massive welfare state with tens of trillions of dollars of wealth transfer over 50-odd years won't do it. Affirmative action won't do it. Even electing a black president won't do it, because original sin demands a complete revolution of spirit and place that affects every aspect of society and the plucking out of sin from every human soul.

The fact that slavery was part of American society in the eighteenth century is certainly problematic. It was a major controversy at the time of the nation's founding and remained so. But slavery has been part of every civilization in human history. Why is it the "original sin" of the United States, for instance, and not Brazil, or Benin, or every country in the world? Mauritania decriminalized slavery in 2007, though hundreds of thousands of black Mauritanians are still born into a system of hereditary chattel slavery in which Arabs own them. But if America uniquely bears the stain of the sin, does that include all Americans—or just the white ones?

Obama's vision of America still stained by "original sin" in 2008, taken to its logical conclusion, winds up exactly at the same place that America found itself a decade later, when Black Lives Matter activists, the *New York Times*' "1619 Project," and critical race theorists were demanding the wholesale abolition of whiteness and the complete restructuring of American society around the idea that it is shot through with racism at every level. There is a throughline from Obama's defense of Jeremiah Wright's lunatic ramblings, and his claim that America today is stained with the guilt of the original sin of slavery, to the George Floyd riots of the summer of 2020 and the ongoing demand that the nation's police be defunded.

"To be antiracist is a radical choice in the face of history," explains noted antiracist theorist Ibram X. Kendi, "requiring a radical reorientation of our consciousness." Kendi, the celebrated author of *How to Be an Antiracist* and a former Boston University professor, often says that the main problem in America is racist policies, rather than individual racists, but at the same time writes, "like fighting an addiction, being an antiracist requires persistent self-awareness, constant self-criticism, and regular self-examination."[3] Antiracism, in Kendi's world, is not a question of not being racist—it is to recognize that one's entire consciousness is a false-hood in need of perpetual pricking, like a religious penitent who wears an itchy undershirt to stay abreast of how evil he is.

This drumbeat of propaganda about race and racism has fueled a massive effort by the Left to remake society, especially the criminal justice system. The 2024 victory of Donald Trump is a setback for the chaos agents, but when leftists retreat it is just to catch their breath and prepare for their next push. As we shall demonstrate in this chapter, their struggle continues, especially in blue cities and states.

In January of 2023, news and rumors began to emerge of some-thing vicious and horrible that had happened in Memphis, Tennessee, regarding the death of a local citizen at the hands of the police. The city seemed desperate to get ahead of the news in the hopes of chilling potential unrest, and warned the public that the forthcoming release of bodycam video would be savage. Crucially, the city fired five police officers and charged them with murder.

Indeed, the video of the arrest and beating of Tyre Nichols was as horrible as foretold. Nichols, who was black, was pulled over for reckless driving, and seems to have run away. The exact circumstances of the traffic stop seem uncertain, but the officers clearly brutalized Nichols, giving him contradictory instructions and beating him without mercy even after he was handcuffed. Tyre Nichols had no criminal record, worked a regular job, and was evidently a devoted son and father. He died in the hospital three days after the vicious arrest.

It's no wonder the city—and the country—braced for vio-lence. Less than three years before, the death of George Floyd in police custody in Minneapolis had sparked massive protests and riots that roiled the country. Billions of dollars of damage were inflicted on cities through arson and looting. Anarchist rabble calling themselves "antifascists" attacked police stations and federal courthouses. Tens of thousands of police officers were injured, and 19 people died in relation to the riots.

The proximate cause of the 2020 riots was the arrest of George Floyd—a violent career criminal who was passing a counterfeit twenty-dollar bill in a convenience store. Floyd was conked out in his car, blasted on drugs, when police officers encountered him. In the ensuing effort to question and arrest him, Floyd apparently had a drug-induced panic attack and demanded to lie down. While being restrained with a conventional police technique, he lost consciousness and died.

The image of George Floyd, who was black, lying on the pavement handcuffed, while a white police officer apparently choked the breath out of him with his knee, created a tableau that millions of people read as emblematic of daily life for African Americans. Al Sharpton, who was instrumental in fomenting deadly riots in New York City in the 1980s and 1990s, announced, "George Floyd's story has been the story of black folks. We could never be who we wanted and dreamed to be as you kept your knee on our neck. It's time for us to stand up in George's name and say, 'Get your knee off our necks!'"[4] This kind of rhetoric can't be held responsible for the violence that spread across the country, but when boosted by hundreds of other major cultural figures and amplified by 24-hour media reporting, it certainly didn't help matters.

The trial of Derek Chauvin, incidentally, was a disgrace and the verdict against him for "killing" George Floyd surely deserves to be overturned. The circumstances of the trial made it impossible for Chauvin to receive due process. Key evidence was suppressed.[5] The courthouse where the trial was held was surrounded by fencing and barricades to guard it against angry mobs, less than a year after the city of Minneapolis had been torched by rioters. A juror was found to have participated in George Floyd-related protests, and Congresswoman Maxine Waters showed up near the end of the trial and demanded "more confrontation" if Chauvin were not found guilty. Moreover, prosecution witnesses from the police lied about the applicability and legality of the restraint technique Chauvin used on Floyd.

But Derek Chauvin is unlikely ever to get a fair review of his conviction and faces decades in prison, assuming he isn't murdered there. There are murmurs that he ought to be pardoned, but even if he were to receive a pardon for his federal civil rights conviction, it is unlikely that any governor from Minnesota would ever pardon him for his murder convictions.

When the city of Memphis announced a week ahead of time that the video of Tyre Nichols' death would be released on the Friday afternoon preceding two major NFL conference championships, mayors and governors around the country held their breaths and prayed that calm would prevail. They needn't have worried. Though the footage was objectively far more brutal than the George Floyd video, the fact that all the officers involved in beating Nichols to death were also black apparently neutralized popular discontent. There were some local protests but nothing serious or destructive. Black police abusing someone, evidently, don't cause riots.

White-on-black violence, especially when conducted by the police, carries special significance in American political and cultural life, and it's certainly understandable why there is a lot of sensitivity around the issue, given the history of legal racism in this country. Some pundits and agitators, annoyed that the death of Tyre Nichols hadn't resulted in riots and arson, tried to explain that, regardless of the skin color of the actual officers involved, white racism was still to blame. Then-Representative Cori Bush of Missouri, a member of the hard-Left congressional "Squad" who cut her teeth leading riots in Ferguson after the high-profile shooting of Mike Brown in 2014, explained that "merely diversifying police forces will never address the violent, racist architecture that underpins our entire criminal legal system. The mere presence of Black officers does not stop policing from being a tool of white supremacy."

Jamaal Bowman, another former "Squad" congressman who represented part of the Bronx and Westchester County in New York, mourned that "Tyre Nichols should be alive today. Instead, like so many others he was killed by police. Killed by white supremacy. Killed by America."[6] Suave CNN commentator Van Jones insisted, "The police who killed Tyre Nichols were Black. But they might still have been driven by racism."[7] (In May of 2025, the three Memphis police officers who were tried for the murder of Tyre Nichols—two other officers involved pleaded guilty—were acquitted of all charges. There were no riots or civil unrest.)

But Van Jones's perspective, which can broadly be characterized as a version of "critical race theory," has become rooted in the outlook of many influential people. "Whiteness," according to this point of view, is a force that makes itself felt everywhere but can be pinned down nowhere—like phlogiston or miasma. Like "spooky action at a distance," as Einstein described quantum entanglement.

For instance, in 2019, two boys of South Asian descent harassed a group of black girls at a high-school football game in a New Jersey suburb. In addition to calling them racist slurs, the boys peed on at least one of the girls.

Sounds pretty bad, but the big surprise only emerged when esteemed Princeton historian Nell Irvin Painter explained in the pages of the New York Times that whiteness was to blame, even though none of the parties was white. "While it's tempting to see the reported ethnicity of the boys suspected in the assault as complicating the story and raising questions about whether the assault should be thought of as racist," explained Painter, "I look at it through a different lens. Instead of asking what the boys' reported racial identity tells us about the nature of the attack, we should see the boys as enacting American whiteness through anti-black assault in a very traditional way."[8]

There is no agency for non-white Americans in this framework, and probably not much for whites, either. The United States, it seems, is peopled by puppets animated by the spirit of white supremacy. As Professor Painter says, "the heritage or skin color of the boys suspected of the assault doesn't matter. What matters is that they were participating in this pattern and thus enacting whiteness in a very traditional way." Whiteness is the unseen sea in which we swim—the force that, like gravity, invisibly shapes our world and determines every relation.

The commentators who were disappointed that the Tyre Nichols case didn't provoke riots and violence—the "language of the unheard," as Martin Luther King is frequently quoted as saying—speak to a radical vision of the function of policing in American society. Academics, esteemed jurists, op-ed writers, grant-making foundation executives, and elected officials have all reached consensus on the idea that America is thoroughly riddled with racism, to the extent that every aspect of the country is shot through with white supremacy and a barely disguised compulsion to control black people. The police, they explain, are the frontline agents of repression. It makes no difference what race the individual officers are.

This is a subtle lesson, worthy of a graduate seminar, which is maybe why people failed to riot over Tyre Nichols. After all, the previous decade had been dedicated to instructing America that the problem is when white cops abuse black people—or "melanated bodies," in the words of New York City Public

Advocate Jumaane Williams.[9] Getting people to understand that the problem is structural, or "systemic," cannot be accomplished overnight.

But the idea that the police are inherently racist, regardless of the specific demographic profile of any individual officer, has become received wisdom. And it was this perspective that fed the "Defund the Police" movement, which gained enormous traction starting in 2020. Defund the Police was a national movement, springing seemingly out of nowhere, that demanded the reallocation of municipal resources away from policing and incarceration and toward social services.

The Defund movement has its roots in the most radical precincts on the Left, in police and prison abolitionism. The abolitionist movement contends that the police function as protectors of property and enforcers of the racist dogma that defines policing. Bestselling books like *The New Jim Crow* (2010) by Michelle Alexander and popular films like *13th* (2016) by Ava DuVernay propounded the piquant, but historically inaccurate, thesis that slavery in America never really went away—it was just disguised in the robes of the rule of law.

The Thirteenth Amendment to the Constitution, which outlawed slavery, was ratified in 1865, the same year that the Civil War ended. Seven hundred thousand troops from both sides died in the war, mostly from disease. Tens of thousands died in prison camps, and tens of thousands more lost limbs. Eight percent of all white men between the ages of 13 and 43 were killed in the war between the states, which may not have started out as a war to free the slaves, but it unquestionably ended as one.

Generations of Americans who were raised to believe that the Civil War was a noble fight for the extension of human freedom would be surprised to learn from radical historians such as Michelle Alexander and Ava DuVernay that the real purpose of the Thirteenth Amendment was to continue the peculiar institution, and in fact to extend it to the North.

The text of the short amendment explains that "Neither slavery nor involuntary servitude, except as a punishment for crime whereof the party shall have been duly convicted, shall exist within the United States, or any place subject to their jurisdiction."

The amendment may sound clear enough, but the subordinate clause is the tricky part: "except as a punishment for crime." This, according to prison abolitionists, is the loophole through which slavery was smuggled into post–Civil War America, and has caused as much or more suffering than its original form. The police, too, are implicated in slavery, because, according to the National Association for the Advancement of Colored People, "The origins of modern-day policing can be traced back to the 'Slave Patrol.'" Bands of whites in the American South were deputized as slave patrollers to catch runaway slaves; modern police forces such as the NYPD or LAPD are just slave patrols with nicer uniforms.[10]

This argument doesn't account for how cities in non-slave states formed police departments. Massachusetts abolished slavery in 1783, yet Boston managed to organize an official police department in 1854, modeled after the Metropolitan Police Service in London. California never had legal slavery, yet Los Angeles formed its police department in 1869, never having had any slave patrols to build upon.

"Defund" was not a metaphor. Congresswoman Rashida Tlaib explained in 2021, "Policing in our country is inherently and intentionally racist . . . I am done with those who condone government-funded murder. No more policing, incarceration, and militarization. It can't be reformed."[11] In June 2020, Kamala Harris told MSNBC, "Part of what we have to do here is also look at the militarization of police departments and, and the kind of money that is going to that. And we need to demilitarize police departments."[12] She praised Eric Garcetti, then mayor of Los Angeles, for moving money away from the LAPD and toward social services.

Congresswoman Alexandria Ocasio-Cortez captured the spirit of Defund when she was asked, "What does an America with defunded police look like to you?" She answered, "It looks like a suburb." She continued:

> Affluent white communities already live in a world where they choose to fund youth, health, housing, etc., more than they fund police. These communities have lower crime rates not because they have more police, but bc they have more resources to support healthy society in a way that reduces crime.
>
> When a teenager or preteen does something harmful in a suburb (I say teen bc this is often where lifelong carceral cycles begin for Black and Brown communities), White communities bend over backwards to find alternatives to incarceration for their loved ones to "protect their future," like community service or rehab or restorative measures. Why don't we treat Black and Brown people the same way? Why doesn't the criminal system care about Black teens' futures the way they care for White teens' futures? Why doesn't the news use Black people's graduation or family photos in stories the way they do when they cover White people (eg Brock Turner) who commit harmful crimes?
>
> Affluent White suburbs also design their own lives so that they walk through the world without having much interruption or interaction with police at all aside from community events and speeding tickets (and many of these communities try to reduce those, too!)

Just starting THERE would be a dramatically
and radically different world than what we are
experiencing now.[13]

I quote this at length because it is so richly packed with all
the myths about policing, crime, race, resources, and "services"
in America today. AOC isn't the only one to make this counter-
intuitive statement about suburbs, the idea being that nonwhite
inner cities are effectively occupied military zones, where police
constantly monitor and interfere with residents' lives, criminal-
izing normal behavior. In white areas, on the other hand, people
are allowed to come and go and do as they please without the
threat of surveillance and criminalization.

This is dogma among police abolitionists and leftist criminal
justice analysts.

It's true that if you wander through an upscale suburb—say,
Bethesda, Maryland, or Scarsdale, New York—you are unlikely to
see many police. Daanika Gordon, a Tufts University sociologist
who wrote *Policing the Racial Divide: Urban Growth Politics and the
Remaking of Segregation*, compares police response between afflu-
ent, whiter neighborhoods and poorer, blacker neighborhoods:

I find, perhaps unsurprisingly, that policing in these
districts is very different. In the former, the police act as
responsive service providers. They are quick, thorough, and
helpful when citizens call, and they work collaboratively
with residents and business owners to solve local problems.

In the latter, the police focus on intervening in violence.
They do so through tactics like investigatory stops, which
many see as aggressive, intimidating, and overbroad. In
addition, the high volume of 911 calls in this district means

that patrol officers are stretched thin, and citizens have to
wait longer for a response to their emergencies.

These dynamics reflect a common pattern in which
predominantly Black neighborhoods are simultaneously
over-policed when it comes to surveillance and social control,
and under-policed when it comes to emergency services.[14]

In the white areas, police are helpful and act as "responsive service providers." Gordon doesn't explain what "local problems"
the people have in those districts, only that the police are obliging
in fixing them.

But in black neighborhoods, the police focus on "intervening in violence" and fail to offer rapid response to emergencies,
much less function as responsive service providers. All they do
is respond to 911 calls. In the white neighborhoods, the police
do not focus on intervening in violence, and so one assumes the
violent behavior is allowed to spread and intensify until it passes,
or the violent offenders get tired.

And, critically, black communities suffer both from having
too many police, *and* not enough police.

Adrienne Adams, as speaker of the New York City Council,
made a similar point during her 2025 "State of the City" address:
"Healthy communities are those with investments," Adams
explained. "It is no surprise, then, that neighborhoods experiencing high levels of violence are the least likely to have access to
resources needed for healing and stability."[15]

The progressive logic regarding the origin of crime radically confuses cause and effect. "Safe" neighborhoods are safe
because they have a lot of services, resources, and investment.
Therefore, "unsafe" neighborhoods need more services. Once
these neighborhoods are sufficiently resourced, they will stop
being crime-ridden. The police, as an institution shot through

with racism, have been indoctrinated to approach problems in black neighborhoods from a perspective of stopping violence with the use of violence.

Why do the police spend so much time answering emergency calls for help and focus on intervening in violence in poor black neighborhoods? Gordon implies that this is all part of a plan to criminalize black people and protect white people, but in reality, the police go where the calls are. Just because some neighborhoods have disproportionately more crime than others, that doesn't mean it's a case of "disparate impact" of a badly conceived policy rooted in racism. Nobody divided up black and white people and said, "You blacks go live in the violent neighborhood; we are putting whites over here, in the safe neighborhood."

Neighborhoods do not exist independently of the people in them.

Progressive critics of the police try to dodge the question of why so many emergency 911 calls come from poor, nonwhite neighborhoods, if it is true that white and nonwhite neighborhoods have similar levels of actual criminal behavior, if not arrests. One inventive explanation is that the calls are being made by white gentrifiers who are uncomfortable with the vibrant street life of the communities they are settling. Put out by an unfamiliar culture that they interpret as hostile, they call the police, much as earlier generations of white frontier settlers may have called in the cavalry.

The metaphor is not mine. Georgetown University law professor Paul Butler, the author of *Chokehold: Policing Black Men,* explains that "the way that a lot of African American and Latino people experience gentrification is as a form of colonization. The gentrifiers are not wanting to share—they're wanting to take over."[16]

This is a common perspective in the analysis of race relations in urban America. Nonwhite residents are featured as the original inhabitants, indigenous to their neighborhoods. White people who move in are interlopers, colonizing what does not belong to them and using the power of the state to displace the people who were there first. The Community Service Society of New York, a longtime and well-respected nonprofit organization that focuses on helping the poor, used similar language in its 2019 report "New Neighbors and the Over-Policing of Communities of Color." Explaining that 311 calls, which register nonemergency complaints, disproportionately originate in "either racially diverse or gentrifying neighborhoods of New York City," the report contends that:

> these complaints can lead to an increased police presence,
> which is not merely a consequence of neighborhood change,
> but also a powerful tool for incoming, affluent residents to
> re-define how a community operates and regulate access
> to public space . . . low-income New Yorkers of color are
> generally more likely to avoid contacting the police because
> they feel it would have made them feel less safe.[17]

The weaponization of "safety" has been key to the Left's war against the police. The phrase "public safety" is so powerful in a society where crime is an actual concern for many people that the Left has sought to hijack it. One way they have perverted the meaning of safety is by propagating the myth—really, a hoax—that black people justifiably fear the police, because the police unjustly murder so many black people.

In late May of 2020, an intriguing interaction took place in New York's Central Park. A white woman named Amy Cooper had her dog off its leash, to the annoyance of a black man, Christian Cooper (of no relation), who claimed the dog was frightening the birds he wanted to look at. By Christian's admission, he told Amy,

"Look, if you're going to do what you want, I'm going to do what I want, but you're not going to like it," which she took as a threat. In response, she called 911 and told the dispatcher that an African American man was threatening her.

Christian Cooper filmed the exchange, and it quickly went viral on social media, to enormous outrage that, in hindsight, appears to have primed the public for the hysteria that attended the death in police custody of George Floyd that very same day. The premise of the anger against Amy Cooper was that a white woman reporting a black man to the police is likely to result in his death.

New York City Public Advocate Jumaane Williams held a press conference outside Central Park, where he wept, called for Amy Cooper's arrest, and suggested that had Christian Cooper not filmed the encounter, he would likely have been in prison if not dead. Williams spoke of "the risks of calling law enforcement on a black man" and demanded the arrest and prosecution of Amy Cooper, a white woman "comfortable in her own privilege," who had called the police after being threatened by a black man in Central Park.[18]

Socialist New York City councilmember Tiffany Caban has dismissed subway violence as a "one-in-a-million event."[19] She and Mayor Zohran Mamdani, who was a state assemblyman at the time, counsel people who are in the middle of an escalating, one-sided confrontation not to call the police but to become "Upstanders," distracting violent criminals by "spilling your soda," or asking whether they went to your high school.[20]

This has become common advice. An organization called "Right to Be" began life as Hollaback!, a group that opposed catcalling and sexualized street harassment of women. Right to Be explains that "sometimes people wonder: 'Can I Delegate the police to intervene in harassment?' Our response is that you should *not* contact the police unless you've checked with the person being harassed and they've explicitly asked you to call the police on their behalf."[21] Calling the police is so dangerous that even victims' rights organizations are against it.

In 2023, a pregnant nurse named Sarah Comrie, heading home after finishing her twelve-hour shift at Bellevue Hospital in Manhattan, approached a row of docked rental Citi Bikes, upon which a group of black youths were lounging. She rented one with her phone, undocked it, and was accused of taking it from one of the youths, who pushed it back into its slot. In an ensuing struggle, one of the group began filming as Comrie tried to take the bike and yelled for help. At one point, exasperated, she made frustrated crying noises and was accused of "fake crying."

This kerfuffle became national news because of the potent imagery of a white woman "pretending" to be harassed by black youths and thereby trying to get them killed. Ben Crump, a lawyer who makes a living suing people over "civil rights" violations, posted on Twitter, "This is unacceptable! A white woman was caught on camera attempting to STEAL a Citi Bike from a young Black man in NYC. She grossly tried to weaponize her tears to paint this man as a threat. This is EXACTLY the type of behavior that has endangered so many Black men in the past!"[22] Crump later deleted this post.

The Young Turks, a leftist streaming political commentary show with millions of followers, amplified this sentiment with a segment on the case titled, "Karen Weaponizes White Tears to Hijack Black Man's E-Bike."[23] The idea that a weeping woman being victimized by a group of young men is the perpetrator of violence sounds absurd, but the concept of "white tears" as intrinsically false and threatening became current in the peak Black Lives Matter era, which spanned approximately from 2010 to 2024.

Ruby Hamad's 2019 book *White Tears/Brown Scars* asks how it is "that we have been so conditioned to prioritize the emotional comfort of white people?"[24] In her bestselling book *White Fragility*, Robin DiAngelo, antiracist trainer and mystic soothsayer of self-loathing white liberals, suggests that "white fragility is not weakness . . . it is a powerful means of white racial control and the protection of white advantage."[25] DiAngelo's wider argument is that white people find even "minimal stress" to be so "intolerable" that they effectively throw tantrums whenever they encounter it.

Regarding the actual threat that an encounter with the police will result in the murder of an innocent black person, the numbers are wildly and intentionally overstated. The police kill very few people every year, especially considering the tens of millions of interactions that occur between the public and the police. But you wouldn't know it by talking to leftists. A 2019 survey by the Skeptic Research Center found that 44 percent of self-described liberals believed that the police killed at least 1,000 unarmed black men that year.[26] Eight percent of "very liberal" respondents estimated the correct number as at least 10,000.

In fact, as the *Washington Post* has carefully tracked for several years, police kill about 1,000 people, of all races and sexes, each year, and the vast majority of those are armed and brandishing or firing their weapons.[27] About a quarter of police homicides involve black people, which is higher than their proportion of the population but within range when you consider the higher rate of serious criminality by African Americans.[28] The real number of unarmed black men killed by the police in the United States every year is typically around fifteen.

In the warped logic of progressive criminology, crying is a weapon, calling the police is legalized race murder, and "white fragility"—the supposed panic and anxiety that grips white people when they lose their privilege—is a form of reasserting racial control. This is the context in which calling the police—or even just calling for help—has been purposely distorted into a hostile, vicious act that undermines public safety rather than enhancing it.

Michelle Wu, the mayor of Boston, is a prominent spokesperson for this thesis. At a March of 2025 House hearing on sanctuary cities, she told Republican lawmakers who were skeptical about Boston's sanctuary policy regarding criminal aliens, "If you want to make us safe, pass gun reforms. Stop cutting Medicaid. Stop cutting cancer research. Stop cutting funds for veterans. That is what will make our cities safe." Every public policy except policing makes people safe, according to Mayor Wu.

That same week, Boston resident Lemark Jaramillo, armed with a knife, chased two people into a Chick-fil-A restaurant in the Copley Square neighborhood, attempting to stab them. An off-duty Boston police officer ordered Jaramillo to drop his weapon and shot him when he refused. Jaramillo died. Mayor Wu appeared on television later that evening to express sorrow for the loss of the attempted murderer's life. "My condolences and my thoughts are with the individual whose life has been lost," she mourned. "And I'm also thinking of all of the people who were impacted here today in one of the busier parts of the city with this tragedy."

So, Mayor Wu's sense of what constitutes "safety" may be a little askew.

In sum, the Left has exploited white racial guilt to promote the idea that the police are just slave catchers with updated uniforms and weapons, and moreover, their work is ineffective. The very idea of using police to prevent crime, along this line of thinking, is futile if not stupid. Criminologist and Mamdani advisor Alex Vitale, in his book *The End of Policing*, summarized the perspective:

We don't have to put up with aggressive and invasive
policing to keep us safe. There are alternatives. We can
use the power of communities and government to make
our cities safer without relying on police, courts, and
prisons. We need to invest in individuals and communities
and transform some of the basic economic and political
arrangements in our society. Chemical dependency, trauma,
and mental health issues play a huge role in undermining
the safety and stability of neighborhoods. People who are
suffering need help, not coercive treatment regimes or self-
help pabulum; they need access to real services from trained
professionals using evidence-based treatments.[29]

The people who want to "defund" the police—a polite way
of saying "castrate" or "abolish"—don't paint a picture of a law-
less society where the strong take what they want, and people of
means hire private security, as they do in many parts of Latin
America and other developing regions without firm rule of law.
Call it frontier justice, street justice, or Mafia-style enforcement
of the peace, there's always going to be some form of policing, like
it or not.

No, the advocates of Defund offer a vision of a harmonious
society, where communities work together to help their troubled neighbors. Where the root causes of violence are addressed
through early intervention, including mentoring of gang members by trusted community elders who were once in gangs themselves. Where homelessness is solved by giving people houses,
and drug addiction is cured by providing addicts with safe, clean
spaces to do free drugs under observation, or at least given access
to clean supplies and opioid antagonists in case they overdose.
Where the seriously mentally ill in the midst of a violent melt-
down are calmed by trained social workers and encouraged by

their fellow sufferers to accept treatment. Where schools have class sizes of no more than 12 or 15 students, and classes are taught with cultural sensitivity. Where the people can shop at city-owned grocery stores that offer healthy, local food at cost, and buses and subways run quickly and efficiently for free.

All this could happen easily, if we were only to defund the police.

This utopian fantasy sounds ridiculous on its face, but it is repeated constantly by liberal officials in every major blue city in America—which essentially means every city in America. Getting rid of the police is only half the battle . . . but as we shall see, it's the most important element of the equation.

Crime spiked in the summer of 2020, amidst the George Floyd unrest and the pandemic-related shutdowns, while calls to defund the police surged in major cities. The intuitive and rational response to a rise in street crime—shootings, felony assault, robbery—would be to beef up police presence, but radicals took another approach. It was the police, and all the repressive powers they represent, that were the problem.

This is an old line of thought, perhaps best expressed by the influential nineteenth-century anarchist philosopher Peter Kropotkin, who wrote, "The law has no claim to human respect. It has no civilizing mission; its only purpose is to protect exploitation." What we call "the law" in this perspective is merely a tool of the rich and powerful to control the poor and hopeless. A mill owner whose child workers are malnourished, underpaid, and subject to loss of limb in dangerous machinery is considered a societal model, while one of his employees who steals a loaf of bread could be hanged as a thief.

Zohran Mamdani, incidentally, expressed this sentiment superbly at an October 2021 "Rally to Free Our People" at the Bronx courthouse. This gathering was in protest of the problematic tendency of the Bronx District Attorney's office to prosecute criminals and seek prison sentences when they were found guilty. "Violence is an artificial construction," Mamdani explained. "So, we have to be very clear that what is happening here, with these district attorneys, that is violence."[3]

Kinetic acts of aggression, we must understand, are only called violence because they are construed as such by the agents of power. Actual violence includes things like bail, punishment, poor housing conditions, and large class sizes. Violence, law, justice—these are all abstractions defined by the lords of humanity so they can more effectively squash the necks of the people with their boots.

This radical vision of the real purpose of law and order was somewhat attenuated in the period between 1900 and 1935 by the abolition of child labor, the imposition of health and safety standards, the adoption of a five-day work week, and eventually the legal protection of labor organizing in industry.

There are arguments to this day about who introduced these advancements in the workplace: whether it was government or an enlightened business class that, as with Henry Ford, wanted to retain a trained workforce and cultivate workers who could buy their products, or a rising workers' consciousness that demanded and won improved standards of living, but in either case rising prosperity in America took the wind out of the sails of anarchists who called for the abolition of law as it was understood.

But the idea didn't go away. Indeed, it has a certain absurdist charm: Laws define crime, so if you eliminate law, the crime rate will go to zero! Of course, there is a difference between "crime" and "injury." You can officially eliminate crime without doing anything about a stolen television or the knife sticking out of someone's neck. This is the essence of "anarcho-tyranny," which is the selective prosecution of crime committed by enemies of the regime, and the nonprosecution of crimes committed by its friends.

The radical tendency in criminological politics gained inspiration and new life in the period of global decolonization after World War II, when theories about national liberation, race, and imperialism led to new forms of revolutionary thought. Frantz Fanon, a French psychiatrist from Martinique, theorized in his 1952 classic *Black Skin, White Mask* that colonialism imposes a psychopathology on everyone involved, deforming the consciousness of the colonizer and the colonized. Colonial subjects internalize a sense of inferiority and adopt the perspective of the oppressor, while colonizers repress their guilty conscience and live in a state of paranoia and fear.

In his psychiatric work treating patients on both sides of the Algerian war of independence, Fanon developed his key insight that violence is both a symptom of the psychological harm of colonialism and a potential cure. The colonized individual, fighting back through acts of terror or warfare, sought a means to purge internalized inferiority and reclaim agency. Fanon famously wrote in *The Wretched of the Earth* (1961):

> At the level of individuals, violence is a cleansing force. It frees the native from his inferiority complex and from his despair and inaction; it makes him fearless and restores his self-respect. Even if the armed struggle has been symbolic and the nation is demobilized through a rapid movement of decolonization, the people have the time to see that the liberation has been the business of each and all and that the leader has no special merit. . . .

> Europe is literally the creation of the Third World.
> The wealth which smothers her is that which was stolen
> from the underdeveloped peoples. The ports of Holland,
> the docks of Bordeaux and Liverpool were specialized in
> the Negro slave trade, and owe their renown to millions of
> deported slaves. So when we hear the head of a European
> state declare with his hand on his heart that he must come
> to the aid of the poor underdeveloped peoples, we do
> not tremble with gratitude. Quite the contrary; we say to
> ourselves: "It's a just reparation which will be paid to us."[31]

Europe is the creation of the Third World, the same way that America is a creation of its slaves, the productive steal from the poor, and—as will be discussed in a later chapter—white suburbs extract wealth from nonwhite inner cities.

Fanon did not necessarily advocate the use of violence but analyzed it as a fact of the colonial experience and the anticolonial struggle. He was realistic about the collateral damage that violence can do to the psyche of the revolutionary, but in the heady milieu of the Algerian war, his apocalyptic attitude was not exceptional. Other theorists and revolutionaries of the period, including Mao, Che Guevara, Brazil's Carlos Marighella, and Ghana's Kwame Nkrumah, made similar arguments about the necessity of armed struggle, not simply to overthrow the oppressor but as a means of raising the consciousness of the people.

Marighella, a revolutionary Communist who waged urban warfare against the Brazilian regime, insisted in his *Minimanual of the Urban Guerilla* that targeted violence to provoke the government to intensify repression was, "we repeat and insist on repeating: the best way of ensuring public support." Che Guevara, the Argentine doctor who became a leading figure in the Cuban revolution, spoke lovingly of violence as a means of waking the sleeping revolutionary conscience of the masses.

Third World revolutionary violence of the 1960s may seem somewhat removed from debates about arrest statistics in modern American cities, but there is a direct line running from early-twentieth-century revolutions to the "Defund the Police" movement of today. One key data point on that throughline is Angela Davis.

Born in Birmingham, Alabama, in 1944, Angela Davis, went on to become a celebrated Communist activist, an alleged political prisoner, a glamorous symbol of black revolutionary struggle, and a noted theorist of prison abolition—a role she occupies to this day.

Angela Davis grew up in a politically inflected household. Her mother was a member of the Southern Negro Youth Congress, a left-wing civil rights group founded by African American Communists in the 1930s, and Davis grew up surrounded by Communist activists and agitators. She was a Girl Scout at precisely the time that the Girl Scouts were under suspicion for their Communist affiliations. Davis was recruited by the American Friends Service Committee, a left-wing Quaker organization, to participate in a program that brought talented black students from the South to attend integrated schools in the North; Davis chose to attend the progressive Elisabeth Irwin High School in Greenwich Village.

This school, founded by noted education reformer Elisabeth Irwin in 1921, was a finishing school for the children of elite leftists and Communists; its lower school is called The Little Red School House. Among its alumni, the school counts Robert De Niro; Kathy Boudin (founder of the Weather Underground, member of the May 19 Communist Coalition, convicted murderer, and mother of future San Francisco district attorney Chesa

Boudin); the children of executed Communist spies Julius and Ethel Rosenberg; Toshi Seeger, wife of Pete Seeger, noted leftist folk singer, Communist fellow traveler, and activist; and Ronald Radosh, famous ex-Communist. As a high-school student, Davis was recruited into Advance, a Communist youth group, by Bettina Aptheker, daughter of historian Herbert Aptheker, a member of the National Committee of the Communist Party of the United States of America (CPUSA). The school employed many black-listed Communists during the post-war period.

You may have noticed my repetition of the word "Communist" in the previous paragraphs, and perhaps you flinched. "Communist" is one of those words that reflects poorly on the speaker, even as it is meant to insult the object of the term. Like another famous epithet, only the people it applies to are allowed to say it. It's bad taste to pejoratively call someone a Communist in polite company, because it smacks of McCarthyite "Red Scare" tactics. Conservatives who insist on calling Zohran Mamdani a Communist because of his overtly redistributionist policies are condescendingly corrected: No, he is a *Democratic Socialist*. People smile, embarrassed at how crude you are to use the term. It's like calling someone an onanist or a blasphemer—What century are you in, anyway?

But the reluctance with which we use the word—even when it is completely accurate, as it is in my usage above—indicates the extent to which Communism hides itself in plain sight in American society. There was a time, up through 1953 or so, when it was legitimate to call out Communism when you saw it, but then, almost overnight, it became the mark of paranoid nut-cases, Birchers, and hoarders of gold and bullets. But it's not like there weren't Communists—there were a lot of them. They may have stopped identifying themselves openly as Communists, but that's where their sympathies lay, and it was easy enough to see the congruence.

Incidentally, the history of American Communism evinces two major fractures. The signing of the Nazi-Soviet Non-Aggression Pact in 1939 shook many Communists, who were astonished that the primary global force against fascism would ally with its very incarnation. Many Communists, though not as many are alleged, left the Party at that time. The next major shock to American Communism arrived in the spring of 1956, with the revelations of Khrushchev's "Secret Speech," which denounced certain excesses of the Stalinist regime. This seven-hour coda to the 20th Communist Party Congress became known as "On the Cult of Personality and its Consequences."

The speech, delivered in February of 1956, rocked hardline Communists with its revelations that Stalin had centered himself over the principles of the Party and "used extreme methods and mass repressions at a time when the revolution was already victorious." What were those extreme methods? Stalin, reported Khrushchev, had "brutally violated Soviet legality" in purging and executing thousands of Party members. He also "minimized the role and military talents of Marshal Zhukov" to give himself more credit for successfully defeating Germany; similarly, Stalin influenced the making of the film *The Fall of Berlin* to imply that he was the hero of the war. "Not Stalin, but the Party as a whole, the Soviet Government, our heroic Army, its talented leaders and brave soldiers, the whole Soviet nation—these are the ones who assured victory in the Great Patriotic War," announced Khrushchev to thunderous applause.[32]

Following these revelations, we have been told, thousands of American Communists were thunderstruck at the news that Stalin was, contrary to widespread belief, not just fallible but evil. Membership in the American Communist Party fell from 20,000 to about 3,000 after Khrushchev's revelations about Stalin. That's the potted version: American Communists were horrified to learn that Stalin was a bad guy, so they quit.

But doesn't it seem like something is missing from this story?

The main thing about the "Secret Speech" is that, while it was delivered in secret, it didn't reveal any secrets. Anyone who had been paying attention to the career of Stalin since the late 1920s would have known he was a madman with a mania for killing not only anyone who had ever known him, but untold millions of others. I am not going to get into the specifics of his crimes, but even revisionist historians of the period who apply the most conservative analyses estimate that Stalin was directly responsible for killing 7 million; other estimates rise as high as 20 million.

American Communists were not so much devastated by Khrushchev's tepid revelations about Stalin as they were by the fact that Stalin, their hero and god, was being posthumously purged from the Party. They saw that the new direction of the Soviet Union was softer and more accommodationist; that the independent socialism of Yugoslavia's Tito was no longer to be viewed as a threat, for example, and that the Soviet Union was likely to pursue accommodation with the West rather than pursue active subversion of its governments. Faced with the prospect of a Soviet Union without Stalin, they cut themselves off from Moscow. They didn't leave the Party, they might have said—the Party left them.

American Communist hardliners only pretended to reject Stalinism. In fact, they disguised themselves as lovers of American liberal democracy and burrowed deep within our institutions: journalism, academia, law and the judiciary, the clergy, and entertainment. From there, they promoted the instantiation of true Communism in the creation of a new constitutional regime, based not on the innate equality of man but on the engineering of society to redistribute its goods and resources according to the ideology of its planners.

They pursued a relentless, subterranean war against the traditional American values of the family, which, according to Friedrich Engels, was the root of capitalist economic structures. They demanded an overturning of all hierarchy and the relentless questioning of sexual mores. They learned to disguise their subversive ideology in the native language of American norms of fairness, in order not to alarm the nation's massive middle class with the language of outright class warfare.

People often say that the targeting of Communists was a "witch hunt." But that's not true. Witch hunts, as a matter of fact, turned up no real witches—but there were plenty of real Communists.

Some stayed behind in the Party, of course, to keep the home fires burning. With her impeccable connections, it's clear that Angela Davis was groomed for greatness in the newer, sleeker Communist Party. And she achieved it. She went to Brandeis University and then Germany, where she studied with noted New Left philosopher Herbert Marcuse, one-time Spartacist revolutionary, member of the Frankfurt School, and major thinker in the field of critical social theory. Marcuse became Davis's mentor, and when she came back to the United States she followed him to UC San Diego to do graduate work. She joined the Communist Party and became active in the Che-Lumumba Club, named for Che Guevara and Patrice Lumumba, the assassinated revolutionary leader of Congo.

Angela Davis was an academic superstar before she had completed a Ph.D., and prestigious institutions vied to hire this twenty-four-year-old grad student, famous for her revolutionary posture, membership in the Communist and Black Panther Parties, and her extravagant hairdo. She identified strongly with Fanon's thesis from *The Wretched of the Earth* and sought to apply his theory of the colonial power structure to the black experience in the United States, seeing the American penal system as a form of internal imperialism.

It was in this heady period of 1969 and 1970 that Davis became involved with George Jackson, one of the notorious "Soledad Brothers" and a cofounder of the Black Guerilla Family Marxist-Leninist prison gang. Jackson, a charismatic sociopath, was serving an indeterminate sentence at California's Soledad State Prison and became a cause célèbre after he and some associates threw a guard off a prison tier, killing him.

Davis began corresponding with Jackson, and they gradually fell in a kind of epistolary revolutionary love. George Jackson was an eloquent if blunt spokesman for the idea that the struggles of black prisoners and the wretched sufferers of colonized people were one. In a June 1970 letter to Davis, Jackson explained that "the secret police (CIA, etc.) go to great lengths to murder and consequently silence every effective black person the moment he attempts to explain to the ghetto that our problems are historically and strategically tied to the problems of all colonial people. This means that they are watching you closely."[33]

Angela Davis did wind up catching the attention of the police a few months later. On August 7, 1970, George Jackson's teenaged brother Jonathan Jackson led an armed group that stormed the Marin County courtroom where a Black Panther prisoner was on trial for murdering a guard. Jackson and his team took hostages, including the judge, and demanded the release of the Soledad Brothers. The gang carried three guns registered to Angela Davis, which she had purchased two days before the attack; she had also been seen the day before in the vicinity of the courthouse with Jonathan Jackson, in the same van that he used in his action. Jackson duct-taped Davis's shotgun to the judge's head and brought him and other hostages to their van. A gunfight broke out in which four people, including the judge and Jonathan Jackson, were killed.

Angela Davis went on the run and lived as a fugitive—listed on the FBI's "Most Wanted" list— for several months before being caught in October 1970. She spent 18 months in jail, during which time she became an international celebrity. Tens of thousands of people around the world formed committees fighting for her freedom; the CIA estimated that 5 percent of all Soviet propaganda in 1971 was directed toward the cause of Angela Davis. John Lennon and Yoko Ono wrote a song called "Angela" on her behalf. The lyrics—perhaps among the ex-Beatle's less inspired— include the forgotten lines:

> Hey, they gave you coffee
> They gave you tea
> They gave you everything
> But equality
>
> Hey, Angela
> They put you in prison
> Angela
> They shot down your man
> Angela
> You're one of the millions
> Of political prisoners
> In the world

While Angela Davis was awaiting trial, George Jackson was killed during an apparent escape attempt, though his supporters insist he was murdered by guards as revenge for the Marin courthouse massacre. Bob Dylan recorded his song "George Jackson" in honor of the dead revolutionary. The song opens:

I woke up this mornin'
There were tears in my bed
They killed a man I really loved
Shot him through the head
Lord, Lord
They cut George Jackson down
Lord, Lord
They laid him in the ground

Protest songs in honor of terrorists and murderers were hot back then. Angela Davis was the "Sweet Black Angel" of the Rolling Stones' track on their classic 1972 album *Exile on Main Street*. Mick Jagger sang, in a West Indian lilt and using a kind of Jamaican patois:

She countin' up de minutes
She countin' up de days
She's a sweet black angel, woh
Not a sweet black slave

Ten little niggers
Sittin' on de wall
Her brothers been a fallin'
Fallin' one by one

For a judge they murdered
And a judge they stole
Now de judge he gonna judge her
For all dat he's worth

These were the days, remember, when Joni Mitchell wore blackface and said her alter ego was a black pimp named "Art

Nouveau." In 1972, John and Yoko went on *The Dick Cavett Show* to defend their new song, "Woman Is the Nigger of the World." The only critics of the song, said Lennon, were "white and male." So, Mick Jagger's exercise in minstrelsy wasn't necessarily unusual enough to draw attention; in fact, the song was the B-side to the Stone's top ten "Tumbling Dice."

Angela Davis was acquitted of murder and conspiracy and weapons charges in 1972. Since then, she has lived a charmed life. She toured the Communist world, including Cuba and the Soviet Bloc, where she was celebrated as a hero. She bonded with East German dictator Erich Honecker—the architect of the Berlin Wall and the brains behind the "shoot to kill" border policy regarding escaping civilians. She received the Lenin Peace Prize in 1979; as of this writing, Angela Davis is the last living recipient of this award.

Davis received honorary doctorates to make up for the one she never bothered to finish at UC San Diego. She held guest professorships at various prestigious institutions until settling down at UC Santa Cruz in 1991, joining her old comrade Bettina Aptheker in the Feminist Studies department. That was the same time, facing the dissolution of the Soviet Union, that she left the Communist Party and helped to found the Committees of Correspondence for Democracy and Socialism, a Marxist party that permits cross-membership with the Democratic Socialists of America.

Her professional position has afforded Angela Davis a comfortable perch from which to continue promoting a hard-left radical agenda. She is credited with introducing the idea and terminology of the "prison-industrial complex" and has worked over the last three decades to communicate the principle of abolition of the "carceral state." Davis cofounded the organization Critical Resistance, which works nationwide to organize protests in favor of the abolition of the police and an end to prisons.

Davis even squeezed in time in 1977 to phone her "friend Jim Jones and all my brothers and sisters from Peoples Temple" in a speech that was amplified live to the Jonestown camp, where, a year later, almost a thousand people would die in a mass murder-suicide. Davis helped juice up Jim Jones's paranoia, affirming to him and his followers that "there is a conspiracy. A very profound conspiracy designed to destroy the contributions which you have made to our struggle . . . we know you are going to win, and in the final analysis, we are all going to win."[34]

A little more than a year after Angela Davis cheered on the residents of Jonestown, Jim Jones and his inner circle forced his primarily black American followers to poison their own children first, so that in their grief and horror at having killed their children they would more readily go along with killing themselves. Angela Davis has never offered any comment on her support for Jim Jones and his cult, nor has she ever expressed public regret over encouraging his paranoid delusions.

Angela Davis is celebrated as the *éminence grise* of the contemporary far Left and is frequently cited by its vanguard as an inspiration. She was an honorary cochair of the massively successful 2017 Women's March that launched the anti-Trump "#Resistance"; T-shirts reading, "Angela Taught Me" were seen on college campuses around the country. She was hailed as a visionary and the presiding genius of the Black Lives Matter movement, and her keynote address at the Women's March called for total spectrum resistance to Trump's agenda. "We dedicate ourselves to collective resistance," she proclaimed. "Resistance to the billionaire mortgage profiteers and gentrifiers. Resistance to the healthcare privateers. Resistance to the attacks on Muslims and on immigrants. Resistance to attacks on disabled people. Resistance to state violence perpetrated by the police and through the prison industrial complex."[35]

Much of today's "Defund" rhetoric, and even the specific arguments about "slave patrols" and the Thirteenth Amendment made by Michelle Alexander in *The New Jim Crow* and Ava DuVernay in her film *13th* were originated and popularized by Angela Davis. In *Are Prisons Obsolete?* (2003) Angela Davis writes of "the historical links between U.S. slavery and the early penitentiary system," observing further that "prison regulations were, in fact, very similar to the Slave Codes—the laws that deprived enslaved human beings of virtually all rights. Moreover, both prisoners and slaves were considered to have pronounced proclivities to crime." She concludes that "the persistence of the prison as the main form of punishment, with its racist and sexist dimensions, has created this historical continuity between the nineteenth- and early twentieth-century convict lease system and the privatized prison business today."[36]

As a Marxist-Leninist by training, Angela Davis always seeks to contextualize local conflicts in terms of global struggle. This is key to Communist thought and practice, because it orients individuals toward seeing themselves as part of a sweeping historical narrative and gives meaning to otherwise mundane and depressing aspects of life.

That's why popular mottos like, "Think globally, act locally" are so insidious. "Acting locally" is sensible, because people can look around themselves and their communities and arrive at a reasonable determination of "What is to be done?" as Vladimir Lenin asked in his 1902 book of that title. But "thinking globally" demands that you place your local action in a wider context, rooted in an overriding ideology.

So, for instance, it becomes a matter of urgency for Americans to stop using fossil fuels, because their combustion leads to climate change, even though developing economies will continue to burn oil and coal without regard for carbon capture and in quantities that dwarf our expensive efforts to transition to wind and solar energy. Well, that's just a matter of us setting a good example in "global thinking" for our benighted brothers in Asia and Africa. Kind of like, "We'll commit suicide today, and you can join us tomorrow!"

In any case, Angela Davis has been at the forefront of connecting policing in America both to the history of American chattel slavery and to imperialism and "settler colonialism." For instance, in a 2014 interview called, "Ferguson Reminds Us of the Importance of a Global Context," Davis explains that while she agrees with the thesis of Michelle Alexander's book *The New Jim Crow*, she wishes that the book had positioned the history of American incarceration within the framework of colonial oppression. Her book *Freedom Is a Constant Struggle: Ferguson, Palestine, and the Foundations of a Movement* explicitly argues that American policing not only resembles the Zionist occupation of Palestinian land but in fact is part of the same phenomenon. Davis writes:

> Racism provides the fuel for maintenance, reproduction, and expansion of the prison-industrial complex. And so if we say abolish the prison-industrial complex, as we do, we should also say abolish apartheid, and end the occupation of Palestine!

It's not even clear which of these goals—abolition of prisons or freeing Palestine—takes precedence. It's more like they must be achieved simultaneously.

This is called "enthymemic reasoning," which is an argument that leaves out the middle term. "I am a person; therefore, I will die" omits "all people die," but we can fill it in easily enough. This rhetorical maneuver gets abused when the statement is a non-sequitur, as in "We want to get rid of prisons; therefore, we must erase Zionism!"

A lot of Leftist argumentation is like this. During her 2016 presidential campaign Hillary Clinton declared in Harlem, "We face a complex set of economic, social, and political challenges. They are intersectional, they are reinforcing, and we have got to take them all on." No half measures; all or nothing.[37]

"All struggles are interconnected" is the essence of Critical Race Theory (CRT), stemming from its core insight about "intersectionality." CRT is built around the idea that a black woman suffers not just from sexism and racism separately, but from both at once, which makes it exponentially more complicated. This leads to a hierarchy of oppression and fostered the whole Diversity, Equity, and Inclusion (DEI) industry during the Biden presidency. Though some of the architecture of CRT/DEI is being dismantled, it persists under the surface, like one of those coal seam fires that can burn underground for decades.

The logic of intersectionality is pernicious, because it compels agreement and negates reasoning. Lenin, a master of totalitarian witticisms, said, "Who says A must say B," meaning that if you can convince people to accept certain premises, it's a weak leader who can't force them to accept the next step, and the next, until they have arrived at the pre-arranged consensus that was waiting for them all along.

"Queer liberation means defund the police," tweets Zohran Mamdani. "Free Palestine is a climate justice issue," explains the Climate Justice Initiative. Prism Reports explains that "prison abolition is environmental justice." Gun violence, according to the American Medical Association, is a "public health issue," and so is "structural racism." The ACLU tells us that "trans rights are women's rights," and the League of Conservation Voters reminds us that "climate justice must include LGBTQ+

justice." The Transgender Law Center is even more expansive, letting us know that "Trans justice is migrant justice, disability justice, racial justice, environmental justice, reproductive justice, economic justice, and gender justice. An agenda for trans liberation is a blueprint for liberation for all." Democrat Senator Sheldon Whitehouse, channeling a Maoist struggle session, told the Senate Budget Committee, "Reproductive justice is economic justice. Restricting one restricts the other."

We could do this all day, playing "Six Degrees of Exhortation." Every cause is every other cause, and being a single-issue voter is a form of false consciousness. What is needed is an awakening to the reality that all struggles are one struggle.

Now we arrive at the gist of my digression into radical Communist history and the odd career of Angela Davis, which is to demonstrate how the current movement against the police has a specific genealogy rooted in Third World revolutionary rhetoric. This bloodline, from Che Guevara's and Ho Chi Minh's theories of peasant insurgency and Frantz Fanon's praise of the cleansing power of anti-imperial violence, through Angela Davis's patient efforts to midwife global revolution through the American racial matrix, has its current instantiation in the "Defund the Police" movement of today.

One key example is the "Stop Cop City" crusade. Cop City refers to a police training center being built in Atlanta, which has become an obsessive focus of the hard Left. Officially known as the Atlanta Public Safety Training Center, Cop City sits on eighty-five acres of city land, and when completed it will have classrooms, a shooting range, a "burn building" for firefighters to practice on, and a mock city, of the sort one sees in movies, so the police can train for active shooter situations.

There's nothing especially unusual or pernicious about this facility, but opposition to it has taken on international dimensions.

The American Friends Service Committee explains that "Cop City will allow police not just from Atlanta, but globally, to learn repressive tactics, so that protests and rebellions can be easily crushed." "Stop Cop City" activists calling themselves "forest defenders" occupied the site starting in 2021, building platforms in the trees to live in and destroying earth-moving equipment. The protests escalated until a firefight broke out in January 2023, when a Venezuelan protester, who went by the name Tortuguita ("little turtle"), shot at police officers during a raid on the encampment; Tortuguita was killed in the ensuing battle.[38]

Memorials to Tortuguita have gone up around the country, and he is frequently cited as a victim of white supremacy and the police-industrial complex gone mad. Congresswomen Rashida Tlaib and Cori Bush and Senator Ed Markey have called for an independent investigation into his death. New York, the Bay Area, Chicago, Dallas, and Seattle are among the American cities that have plans to build or expand police training centers, and in each locality a "Stop Cop City" movement has popped up to oppose it. *City Limits*, an urban policy magazine owned by the Community Service Society of New York, warns, "'Cop City' has a new location on its carceral tour: New York City."[39]

On one hand, the "Stop Cop City" movement is another iteration of the Defund the Police movement. But in a sinister turn, the construction of police training facilities has been identified as part of the Zionist project of oppression, displacement, and imperialist death. *The Guardian* quotes Keyanna Jones, a Baptist minister who wears T-shirts reading, "STOP COP CITY FREE PALESTINE," explaining why the two topics are connected to one another. "There are reasons why the movement to stop Cop City and the push for a ceasefire now are related," Jones said. "You have the same Israeli forces in both places . . . and you see the marked militarization. . . . You can't deny it when you see local police officers walking around in riot gear."[40]

This hallucinatory mishmash, seeing Zionist forces everywhere, is actually very common on the anticarceral Left and has been at least since the 2014 Ferguson riots. "You cannot understand what is happening in Palestine unless you understand what is happening in black Atlanta; and you cannot understand what is happening in black Atlanta unless you understand what is happening in Palestine," an activist screams at the beginning of an Al Jazeera video segment called "From Tel Aviv to Cop City: Exchanging Tactics."

The central concern is the Georgia International Law Enforcement Exchange (GILEE), a program through which police forces from around the world train and learn best practices from one another. Such exchanges have been around for decades. Participating nations in GILEE include Brazil, the Bahamas, Canada, the United Kingdom, Hungary, Israel, and many others. But activists have focused solely on Israel and concocted a fiction that virtually every police force in the United States is trained by the Israeli Defense Forces in how to brutalize a local population.

Writers Against the War on Gaza (WAWOG) sponsored a forum titled "Demilitarize Atlanta to Palestine" in February 2024, in Queens, New York. As WAWOG explains:

> The blueprint for Cop City was inspired by Israel's very own Cop City called Little Gaza in an-Naqab or the so-called Negev Desert. Israel's Cop City is built on stolen Palestinian land, and Georgia's Cop City proposed site is the Weelaunee Forest, 381 acres of stolen Muscogee land. This relationship symbolizes the connections between the prison industrial complex, militarism, settler

colonial oppression, white supremacy, and expanded state-sanctioned violence against working-class Black and Indigenous communities. . . .

(Police training facilities have been around since well before the establishment of Israel; simulated towns with pop-up targets date to the 1920s.)

WAWOG continues:

> From Myanmar's ethnocide against the Rohingya and the surveillance of refugees and Indigenous people at the U.S.-Mexico border to India's campaign against Kashmir and slave markets in Libya, Israel has aided, abetted, and continues to profit off violence across the globe. . . .
>
> The U.S. learns tactics and strategies from Israel, who is deemed as a beacon of "successful policing," and in turn, brings those strategies back home to increase criminalization against Black and brown people, surveil Muslims, and repress Indigenous-led movements, to name a few examples. The U.S.'s adaption of Israeli counter-insurgency policing, immigration, and surveillance models reinforces and legitimizes occupation and apartheid in Palestine by the Zionist entity.

This feverish narrative goes on at length; I have provided only the barest snippet. But examples of this trope abound. Protesters in New York chant, "NYPD, KKK, IDF: They're all the same!" and "Move cops, get out the way! We know you're Israeli trained." In Chicago, they substitute "CPD." The *Los Angeles Times* expressed concern that cops from the United Arab Emirates were training at the LAPD academy, but it threw in extra concern that the LAPD "has sent personnel to study and train with Israeli security forces accused of state-sanctioned violence."

Zohran Mamdani has always drawn a straight line between Zionism and the American capitalist police state. At a 2023 Democratic Socialists of America panel discussion, Mamdani explained to the audience, "We have to make clear that when the boot of the NYPD is on your neck, it's been laced by the IDF. . . . We have so many opportunities to make clear the ways in which that struggle over there is tied to capitalist interests over here."[41]

It is essential to the hard Left anti-police Defund narrative that colonialist brutality be a backdrop to everyday policing in a liberal democracy. Casting the police as violently occupying enemy territory—like Israeli occupation of the West Bank or the U.S. Army patrolling "strategic hamlets" in Vietnam—enables the Left to overlay Third World liberation struggles on American racial politics.

It's not enough to seek reform of troubled police departments or discipline for bad officers, because the entire system is as rotten and disgusting as British rule in India or French domination of Algeria. So, gentrification literally becomes settler-colonialism, with black or Latino residents of a poor neighborhood in the role of exploited and displaced indigenous people if white people move in. The insistence, direct from Fanon and Marighella, that the people resist and overthrow a wicked regime in its entirety, is necessary to sustain progressive momentum.

This is what they mean by their shirts reading, "Angela Taught Me." This is her lesson.

SEIZING CONTROL

On the road to global revolution, naturally, the Defunders face a long, thousand-mile journey that begins with a single step.

Though a cleansing uprising that sweeps away all injustice remains a guiding star for the Left, there are many preliminary stages along the way. The tide of purifying violence will assuredly rise, but it is necessary to deal with the table that History has laid for us in the here and now.

One practical—as opposed to ideological—reason the Left is so set on defunding the police is because departments of public safety are one of the only major institutions in America that have not been captured by the Democratic Party and its many allies. Schools, university faculties, health and hospitals, public interest law, the media, much of the judiciary, labor unions, libraries . . . every civic organization of note is staffed and run by liberals, if not radicals. In terms of political donations, conservatives have an edge among retirees and corrections and peace officers.

Even the military, which was long a bastion of traditional masculine values of courage, capability, fraternity, and strength, was quickly turned inside out by the Biden administration. The armed forces conducted a political purge of "white extremists," set minority recruitment and promotion policies, forced everyone to undergo sensitivity training, and endorsed trans ideology. Some of this is being undone in the newly renamed "Department of War," but the entire episode demonstrates how readily subject to capture a massive institution under federal jurisdiction can be.

A big-city Democrat politician looks at the funding that flows automatically every year to the local police department and fumes. The urban political economy depends on feeding money to one's constituents. In the old days, cities were run on the patronage system. Political machines hired party supporters for municipal jobs, and they in turn helped turn out the vote for the preferred candidate. This system was corrupt, but you can't say it wasn't responsive. In New York City, for instance, local political clubs allied to the machine ran the city, but they also took care of their members and the community.

With the advent of the Progressive movement (the old, reformist movement closely associated with Professor Woodrow Wilson, author of the seminal 1887 paper *The Study of Administration*, and later two-term president of the United States), patronage politics was gradually replaced with professional administration of affairs. It makes no sense, said the reformers, to bring in a new cohort of city clerks and garbage men every time there's an election. Better to develop a class of civil servants whose career is to administer public affairs, and who can operate efficiently above the level of mundane, dirty electoral politics. As professionals, these public administrators will consider the long-term needs of the polity rather than the short-term demands of elected officials who, after all, are only concerned with what the voters want.

What this has all resulted in, to cut to the chase, is a system where power in blue cities has shifted away from old-style political machines toward new sources of votes and money. One important arm of this octopus is public-sector labor unions. It used to be the case that public employees were considered unsuitable for unionization because they work for the government, and thus for the taxpayer. Unlike traditional unions, where workers sell their labor to a boss, who seeks to profit from it, public employees do not operate under a profit-seeking model. Even Franklin D. Roosevelt—the architect of the New Deal and the closest thing to a socialist dictator the country has ever seen—believed that:

> All Government employees should realize that the process
> of collective bargaining, as usually understood, cannot
> be transplanted into the public service. It has its distinct
> and insurmountable limitations when applied to public
> personnel management. The very nature and purposes of

> Government make it impossible for administrative officials
> to represent fully or to bind the employer in mutual
> discussions with Government employee organizations. The
> employer is the whole people, who speak by means of laws
> enacted by their representatives in Congress.[42]

Despite FDR's view on the essential contradiction of letting government workers form bargaining units, many cities and states began to recognize bargaining units among their employees, starting in the 1950s. New York City led the way in this movement. Today, when leftist politicians praise labor or call their city a "union town," they are almost certainly talking about government workers. Today, 32.2 percent of public-sector workers belong to a union, versus only 5.9 percent of workers in private industry. About half of all union members in the United States work for government, even though there are five times as many private-sector as public-sector employees.[43]

Public-sector unions engage heavily in local politics. They raise money for candidates and contribute huge amounts of money in elections. They can turn out union members and salaried union officers as "volunteers" for rallies or political canvassing, effectively making massive in-kind contributions to electoral campaigns. The politicians, in turn, cater to the demands of the labor unions and fight like mad to increase spending that will maintain or boost union rolls.

You see the problem: Government workers are paid through taxes, their union takes a portion of that income as dues, which it uses to elect pliable politicians to office, who make sure that tax money continues to flow to the union, whose members work for government. At the negotiating table, labor and management are sitting on the same side of the table, effectively conspiring against the people.

Organized labor used to have the power to bring the nation to a standstill by calling strikes in coal mines, railroads, or factories. But public employee unions don't have to strike to get what they want. Stuffed on dues, public-sector unions have molded local government into a tool whose purpose is to satisfy public-sector union demands.

Police also have unions, of course, but labor activists and other leftist observers don't count police unions in their movement. In 2020, during the Great Awokening of George Floyd/BLM/Covid, the King County Labor Coalition in Seattle voted to expel the police union unless it agreed that policing in general, and the Seattle police in particular, were racist, and committed to undergo racial sensitivity training. In cities around the country, political officials and labor leaders joined forces to demand that police unions agree to stricter discipline of bad officers.

Aside from keeping unions happy, local blue-city government justifies its growth by providing services. What are services? Education, sanitation, public safety, road and bridge infrastructure, and transit are the traditional municipal services that citizens expect from a well-run city. But even those sectors, with all the labor votes they entail, don't hold enough bags to fill with enough taxpayer money to ensure permanent majorities forever. Hence, we have seen the rise of nonprofit organizations offering additional services, and thus bringing in new constituencies.

Nonprofit groups often provide services that you might never have known were needed. New York City has a lot of immigrants. About 40 percent of the population of the city was born abroad, and it is unsurprising that, having started over in a new country, many of them are not wealthy. Every demographic faction has a nonprofit organization that is set up to "serve" the community, and each of them vies for government money to do it. For instance, there is a group called DRUM, standing for "Desis

Rising Up & Moving," which claims to offer the following services, as only a sample of their full menu:

- **South Asian Workers Center.** Educates and assists low-wage workers to access labor rights and address employment discrimination, and runs legal clinics.
- **Gender Justice Program.** Develops leadership of young women to lead gender justice and social change in their homes, schools, and communities.
- **Hate Free Zones.** Builds neighborhood-based community defense systems and community safety mechanisms for all people.
- **Global Justice Program.** Builds coalitions internationally for peace and migrant rights. Supported over 100 community members with referrals to legal service providers, translation, support letters, and/or other case management activities. Supported over 70 women and girls through referrals to services and support networks.[44]

A lot of what DRUM does—as do many of these affinity-based groups—is refer people to services already provided by the government. The rest of it is basically organizing the community to become active participants in DRUM and to engage in local politics, though its tax status as a charitable organization is supposed to prohibit that activity.

DRUM made news during the 2025 NYC mayoral race, coming into its own with its remarkable voter outreach to local Bangladeshis, Pakistanis, and Indians on behalf of Zohran Mamdani. Turnout among these groups exploded and easily provided Mamdani's margin of victory in the Democratic primary. A tax-exempt organization that receives government funding isn't supposed to engage in election work. It's strictly illegal, though these groups routinely establish related entities (e.g., DRUM

Beats) that share office space and staff but are incorporated under a different section of the tax code. This is standard practice among leftist nonprofits, and nobody seems to notice.

But DRUM is also closely connected to Haqooq-e-Khalq, a Communist political party in Pakistan, whose leader, Ammar Ali Jan, celebrated the participation of party members in the Mamdani campaign.[45] New York City tax-exempt community-based organizations legally aren't supposed to coordinate with Third World revolutionary parties to influence local elections, either, but again, nobody seems to notice.

Make the Road is a similar group, focused on Latin American migrants, which receives tens of millions of dollars from the city and state. This is how Make the Road—which has a dozen staffers who earn six-figure salaries—describes its work in its official submission to the IRS:

> High quality legal and health access services, and work
> to change unjust systems through impact litigation,
> policy design, and working side-by-side with members
> and organizers on adoption of those policies. Our legal
> team works in the area of employment, immigration law,
> housing and benefits and TGNCIQ* rights, helping to
> tackle crises like an impending eviction or an order of
> deportation. Our health team works to provide assistance
> so that community members can access healthcare
> services, avoid crushing medical debt and access nutrition.
> Thanks to the trust we build with community members,
> we are often able to avert crises before they spiral out of
> control and ensure that all members of a family get services
> they need to thrive over the long term.

---

* "TGNCIQ," incidentally, refers to "Trans, Gender Non-Conforming, Intersex, and Queer."

Make the Road, like dozens of other groups, mostly advises illegal immigrants about their rights and advises them how best to take advantage of the free healthcare, housing, and legal services that New York City provides. (Despite claims that illegal immigrants are not allowed to take advantage of federally funded benefits such as housing, it is well known that loopholes, including "mixed-status family" and child eligibility, programs partly funded and managed by the state, and transitioning visa petitions permit such abuses of the system.) "Impact litigation" means suing the government—using government funding—on behalf of people who did not get their services quickly enough.

But the real functions of these groups are to swell out crowds at protests, press conferences, and rallies; to march in parades; and to denounce nonsupportive political candidates as racists. The groups work in concert with labor unions, political organizations such as the Working Families Party, and elected officials to cross-promote one another.

This process is sometimes called "capture." Nonprofit groups are "rent seekers," which start out cup in hand, begging for money to expand whatever outreach or training or service provision they claim as their mission. As they grow, however, they become the tail that wags the municipal dog. Elected officials clamor to give these powerful groups money, because these ostensibly nonpartisan organizations exercise enormous political influence.

It's not just in New York. The same thing goes on around the country. In Chicago, for instance, The Resurrection Project collects tens of millions of dollars from the local and state government to organize illegal immigrants, conduct vigils for victims of violence, and provide community-based cover for real estate developers building housing projects. The Resurrection Project also played a role in the recent fraud trial and conviction of longtime Illinois Democrat boss Michael Madigan, who wanted the group to give his son "something."[46]

This digression on nonprofit organizations and the pro-social benefit they purport to provide is deeply relevant to the larger discussion of the police and the effort to defund or abolish them as an institution. As noted earlier,, the police, from the perspective of a progressive elected official, are "useless eaters," as the Nazis called the disabled. They suck up a lot of money and provide nothing in return to the politicians who pass the budgets. And while the Left does maintain its ultimate ideological goal of eliminating the police as a social force, more immediately it would like to shift as much of the public safety budget line to more politically advantageous recipients as possible.

"Gun violence" is a term of art that implicitly, and often explicitly, blames red states for selling guns that cross state lines and magically go off when they reach cities run by liberals. This is a convenient way to shift blame from local leadership, and local gang members, and pin it on gun sellers at the other end of the "Iron Pipeline," as advocates like to call it.

According to liberals, the real answer to most violence, especially the kind of random street violence that really terrifies people, is *services*. Services of all kinds, but especially housing, mental health treatment, peer counseling, violence interruption, midnight basketball, and restorative justice—all the things that nonprofit organizations claim to provide. The prevailing idea behind progressive criminology is that deviance—stealing, raping, killing people—has root causes that are amenable to improvement.

For instance, Chicago Mayor Brandon Johnson chose to discontinue his predecessor Lori Lightfoots's "accountability Mondays," when her staff would gather to analyze weekend violence. "I've been clear about this from the very beginning," Johnson explained in June of 2024. "If we truly want to address the root causes of violence in our communities, we must make lasting, long-term investments in our people."[47]

The word "investment" is often used by progressive politicians to avoid the word "spending," which is more apt.

But Johnson's real point is that "accountability" is the wrong way to look at Chicago violence. No one, least of all Mayor Johnson, should be held accountable for the dozens of shootings that typically happen on a busy Chicago weekend. Blaming him, or even blaming the shooters, is another form of blaming the victim. As he says the "root cause" of violence is the lack of "lasting, long-term investments in our people."

When someone is shot, it's a problem of gun violence. When someone is stabbed, shoved in front of a subway car, or beaten to death, it's usually a failure of mental health and housing policy. In either case, the answer is never, "We need to have more money for policing." It's always, "Look at all the money we waste on the police."

During the Covid lockdown/summer of Floyd extravaganza, when the crime rate spiked, Alexandria Ocasio-Cortez suggested:

> Maybe this has to do with the fact that people aren't paying
> their rent and are scared to pay their rent and so they go
> out and they need to feed their child and they don't have
> money so you maybe have to . . . they are put in a position
> where they feel they either need to shoplift some bread or
> go hungry that night.[48]

Hers is a crude expression of the idea that poverty drives crime, including violent crime. But this appealing idea isn't true. During the Great Depression, when unemployment was 25 percent and many people were going hungry and living in tin shacks, the murder rate in New York City did not rise appreciably. More generally, the homicide rate in the nation's major cities in 1890—at the height of mass immigration and slum living conditions—was much lower than it was 100 years later, by as much as a factor of six in New York, Boston, and Philadelphia. Criminologist Barry Latzer explains that "there is no trend, no consistent relationship, between general economic conditions and violent crime. This anomaly continued after World War II. Violent crime soared during periods of great prosperity, such as the late 1960s, and declined during recessions, such as in 2007–2009."[49]

Nevertheless, politicians and analysts routinely assert that relying on police is the wrong way to address "public safety," which, as Boston Mayor Michelle Wu told Congress, would be better achieved if they would "pass gun reforms. Stop cutting Medicaid. Stop cutting cancer research. Stop cutting funds for veterans. That is what will make our cities safe." The Vera Institute of Justice, among the largest and best-funded think tanks (annual budget: $200 million) focused on criminal justice reform, explains:

> Changing the ways police operate in communities is integral to dismantling systemic racism. Local budgets disproportionately fund police departments over other public services that would promote public safety, including housing, employment support, education, and public health. Using police and punitive approaches as the primary tools to address health and social issues including mental illness, substance use, homelessness, community violence, and poverty funnels millions of people into jails and prisons.[50]

Note the enthymemic logic here: It is a given that "housing, employment support, education, and public health" promote "public safety." And maybe they do, but especially if you expand the definition of *public safety* to mean housing, job support, education, and public health, which is not what most people think of when you say "public safety."

Vera then argues that using the police as the primary tools to address mental illness, substance use, homelessness, community violence, and poverty is a bad idea. But nobody thinks that the police should be the primary tool to address these problems—except in the case of "community violence," which is precisely when people do want to call the police. "Community violence," one assumes, means violence committed by people in the community, on the community—which includes almost all violent crime in America.

Vera repeats a common refrain that "communities should invest in civilian first responder programs for people experiencing behavioral health crises." In this context, "civilian first responder" typically means a social worker or a "peer," a civilian who possesses the *lived experience* of mental health crisis and will thus be able to relate to the suffering individual who prompted the call.

The idea that social workers will be better equipped to handle mental health crises than the police is a shibboleth in this world. Zohran Mamdani's plan for policing in New York City revolves entirely around having social workers handle domestic violence and mental-illness-related 911 calls.

In 2018, the police were called in Brooklyn because a man, Saheed Vassell, was accosting people on the street in the middle of the day and sticking what looked like a gun in their faces. It emerged later that the object was not a gun but a shiny metal pipe, though in security camera footage it certainly looks like a pistol; three separate 911 calls reported that a man with a gun was running around Crown Heights. When the police approached Vassell, he assumed a shooter's stance, pointed his piece of pipe at them, and was shot and killed.

Vassell's family reported that he had been previously diagnosed with bipolar disorder and had received treatment but had not been taking his medication at the time of his death. Clearly a terrible incident. NYPD critics lashed out, insisting that since everyone who knew Vassell well knew he was unstable but harmless, the police ought to have known this as well. Activists called the incident "death by gentrification" and demanded that (white) interlopers "stop calling 911. Blood is on your hands!" In fact, all the people whom Vassell approached with his pretend gun were, like him, black and longtime neighborhood residents.[51]

Jumaane Williams, the public advocate of New York City, has made it his job to insist that social workers be the front line of response to emergencies, which in hindsight turn out to involve distraught mentally ill people. "If we want an effective alternative to police responses to people in mental health crises, we must be meaningfully prioritizing resources for that response," he told the city council in 2024. Williams has also called upon the city to address crises involving violent mentally ill people "holistically . . . as an issue of health, rather than simply law enforcement."

But he's certainly not the only one. Jenny Durkan, the former mayor of Seattle, posted a long thread during the George Floyd riots condemning then-President Trump for criticizing the "free speech" CHAZ (Capitol Hill Autonomous Zone) experiment that barricaded a few blocks of Seattle and forbade the police from entering the area.

Durkan said that CHAZ was a kind of love-in or "block party," though after several shootings and murders and reports of extortion she did send her officers in to restore order. "Seattle is passionate, we demand justice, and I believe we will be at the forefront of true, meaningful change," Durkan tweeted on June 11, 2020. "Nothing will distract our city from the work that needs to be done." The mayor added, "we will continue to fund intervention and mental health programs so that those who call 9-1-1 in crisis are met with the kind of help they really need—whether that is a mental health professional, a social worker, or a community advocate—and not always a police officer."[52]

The idea that the police should be defunded in favor of community-based organizations is standard among Democrat politicians. Gale Brewer, a longtime New York City Council member from the Upper West Side and former Manhattan borough president, has a reputation as a data-driven moderate. In 2021, in response to a candidate questionnaire asking whether she would favor defunding the NYPD, Brewer answered, "Yes, to repurpose toward social workers, violence interrupters, and programs that focus on alternatives to incarceration."[52] There is no demand for evidence that this kind of "root causes" answer works. Rather, it is assumed to be an obvious solution that has been ignored because the police are thirstily draining all the resources.

When people call the police because someone with serious mental illness is having an episode, it's not because the individual is very depressed and withdrawn. It's not because they are crying a lot or sleeping the day away or haven't done the dishes all week.

They are more often behaving along the lines of Saheed Vassell, posing an immediate danger to themselves or others. They may be armed with a knife they refuse to put down, or swinging a bat. People call the police because they need a police response. Most American cities have no shortage of social workers, but social workers don't line up to respond to cases of violent meltdowns, nor are they equipped to do so.

Another progressive panacea to street crime that bypasses the police and contributes funding to community-based organizations is "violence interruption." This idea involves hiring former gang members to counsel youth who are "at risk" of entering a life of crime.

If this sounds suspiciously like a good way for older gang members to recruit new gang members, you'd probably be thinking in the right direction. Violence interrupters monitor social media and keep their ears to the street, listening for the eruption of beefs and squabbles, and then intervene before the shooting starts.

Opportunity Agenda, a nonprofit organization that "looks beyond police to promote true community safety," explains that these interrupter programs "employ local members from the community who have experienced violence themselves to connect with young adults to stop violence before it happens." How does it do this? "After connecting with high-risk individuals, the program links youth with needed services." Again, community-based organizations are paid to direct "clients" to existing services, already funded by the government.[54]

Washington, D.C., has put a lot of resources into its "Cure the Streets" program, which uses "a data-driven, public-health approach to gun violence by treating it as a disease that can be interrupted, treated, and stopped from spreading." The idea of dealing with "gun violence" as a disease or public health crisis is popular among leftist urban policy experts and became widespread during the Obama years. We don't hear about it quite as much since Covid, when the public health authorities suffered a loss of credibility, making the metaphor less useful, but it still comes up frequently.

Cure the Streets, which is run by the Washington, D.C., attorney general, "is based on the Cure Violence Global model, which employs local, credible individuals who have deep ties to the neighborhood in which they work."[55] But who are these "local, credible individuals," how are they identified, and who vets them?

Violence interrupters are a little like confidential informants, in that they are necessarily disreputable individuals who are asked to act as go-betweens. Police assume that their confidential informants might tell partial truths, or rat on rivals, but they accept the shady nature of the relationship because that's how they can acquire inside information that would otherwise be impossible to obtain.

Violence interrupters are usually shady characters, either formerly incarcerated individuals or gang members who have left "the life" and are ready to preach the gospel of clean living to the young guns on the street. But how credible is an ex-gang member to people who are currently gang members? Violence interrupters aren't supposed to be teaching little kids about the golden rule and being polite to their elders; the whole point of the program is for the interrupters to cure violence that is happening now, among the people who are already committed to it.

Briyon Shuford was paid by the D.C. attorney general's office (OAG) to interrupt violence. In early 2025, Shuford was sentenced to 161 months in federal prison for his involvement in an April 2024 drive-by shooting that wounded four people. Shuford's affiliation with the "21st and Vietnam" crew, a notorious gang, did not help his case, nor did selfies he took holding machine guns with illegal high-capacity drum magazines.[56]

Corey Wynn was such a picture-postcard example of someone who had turned his life around that he has a whole page on the OAG website profiling him and telling his story. He was a promising athlete but then took a wrong path and was incarcerated in 2004. "While incarcerated, he made a conscious choice to switch from negative to positive thinking and began to do violence interruption work in whatever way he could," we are told. "He mediated conflicts between inmates and returned items that others had stolen." When C Wynn got out of prison, he joined Cure the Streets and became a full-time Program Supervisor.

When asked what his proudest moment has been in his time with Cure the Streets, he describes a moment where he received a call from a community member about two people arguing. He says it was because of the relationship that Cure the Streets had built with these two individuals that the community felt comfortable calling him to de-escalate the conflict.

A nice story, made for a human-interest segment on local news. But in March of 2025, Wynn was arrested in connection with a 2023 mass shooting in a nightclub that left one person dead and three wounded. Police do not accuse Wynn of being the triggerman; rather, he is believed to have coordinated and overseen the shooting. This, one must note, is the second time he has been implicated in a murder. In 2020—the same time his website profile was posted—he was charged with a 2017 murder, though a judge dismissed the charges, allowing Wynn to go back to interrupting violence, when he wasn't committing it.[57]

Incidentally, while we are speaking of "at-risk youth," in 2019 California passed a law that banned the use, in official documents, of the phrase "at risk" to describe youth identified by social workers, teachers, or the courts as likely to drop out of school, join a gang, or go to jail. Los Angeles assemblyman Reginald B. Jones-Sawyer, who sponsored the legislation, explained that "words matter." By designating children as "at risk," he says, "we automatically put them in the school-to-prison pipeline. Many of them, when labeled that, are not able to exceed above that."[58]

The idea that the term "at risk" assigns outcomes, rather than describes unfortunate possibilities, grants social workers deterministic authority most would be surprised to learn they possess. Contrary to Jones-Sawyer's characterization of "at risk" as consigning kids to roles as outcasts or losers, the term originated in the 1980s as a less harsh and stigmatizing substitute for "juvenile delinquent," to describe vulnerable children who seemed to be on the wrong path. The idea of young people "at risk" of social failure buttressed the idea that government services and support could ameliorate or hedge these risks.

Instead of calling vulnerable kids "at risk," says Jones-Sawyer, "we're going to call them 'at-promise' because they're the promise of the future." The replacement term—the only expression now legally permitted in California education and penal codes—has no independent meaning in English. Usually, we call people about whom we're hopeful "promising." Like someone is a promising ballplayer or a promising poet. Not, "He beat up his grandma and stole a car, but he's definitely 'at promise' of acing the LSAT someday."

The language of the statute is contradictory and garbled. "For purposes of this article, 'at-promise pupil' means a pupil enrolled in high school who is at risk of dropping out of school, as indicated by at least three of the following criteria: Past record of irregular attendance . . . Past record of underachievement . . . Past record of low motivation or a disinterest in the regular school program."[59]

In other words, "at-promise" kids are underachievers with little interest in school, who are "at risk of dropping out."

Without casting these kids as lost causes, in what sense are they "at promise," and to what extent does designating them as "at risk" make them so? This abuse of language is Orwellian in the truest sense, in that it seeks to alter words to bring about change that lies beyond the scope of nomenclature. Jones-Sawyer says that the term "at risk" is what places youth in the "school-to-prison pipeline," as if deviance from norms and failure to thrive in school are contingent on social-service terminology. The logic is backward and obviously naive: If all it took to reform society were new names for things, then we would all be living in utopia right now.

New York City is engaged in a similar project to reshape reality. "EDP calls," the standard designation for emergency police calls involving an "emotionally disturbed person," are now officially called "mental health calls." This change, it's reported, is meant to reduce the stigma associated with calling police when someone is suffering from untreated serious mental illness—as though how the police refer to these calls affects their prevalence or severity.

One of the problems with sticky social problems is that they are hard to budge. This makes the naming of things very important. Getting more kids to graduate from high school is hard, but if we make the standards low, we can graduate more of them. Naming everything in black neighborhoods after black people didn't improve the outcomes for black youth, so let's remove statues of objectionable historical figures.

Public safety is a major consideration for Americans across all demographic subsets. Fear of walking alone at night near one's home reached a three-decade high in 2023, according to Gallup. Since 2021, according to Pew, concerns about crime have grown among self-identified Democrats and Republicans, even as violent crime has supposedly leveled off. Some moderate Democrats have even backed off their fervent demands for the abolition of the police, though many are still holding the course.

The Left are dedicated to capturing the institutions of law enforcement, no matter what they may say at a moment when the public is in favor of policing. They have been seeking to destabilize public order for decades, and there is no reason to expect them to stop anytime soon.

THREE

HOUSING

Racist Roads

In the spring of 2023, Americans were informed of a new mortgage-related initiative by the Biden administration. Beginning in May, they were told, people with high credit scores could expect to start paying a higher amount on their monthly mortgage fees—as much as 1.75 percent more. Meanwhile, people with lower credit scores would get a discount and pay a percentage point less. Borrowers who made minimal down payments—like 5 percent of the purchase price or lower—would also get a bonus reduction in their payments.

This announcement struck most people as strange and contrary to the basic principles of debt management, credit worthiness, and simple financial common sense. Credit bureaus track our bill-paying habits to give lenders a good idea of whether we are likely to pay back money we borrow on time. Having a high credit score means you are a lower-risk borrower, so you would normally be rewarded by getting a lower rate and paying lower fees. Having a low credit score typically means you are higher risk, so banks and other lenders charge you more to borrow money.

Sandra Thompson, the director of the Federal Housing Finance Agency, which promulgated the new rules, explained that the changes would "increase pricing support for purchase borrowers limited by income or by wealth," and would "ensure a level playing field." Critics noted the obvious conclusion that the new rules subsidize lower payments for people with poor credit scores by, essentially, fining borrowers who had made the mistake of soberly managing their personal finances.[1]

Why would the federal government invert the traditional and well-understood standards of credit that have been the basis of American prosperity and in fact have underwritten the capitalist model over the last 500 years? Every meritocratic value we learn as children—about diligence, hard work, delayed gratification, and perseverance in the face of adversity—seems to be tossed in the garbage can with this new initiative, which openly penalizes the thrifty.

To understand why the Biden administration would institute such a perverse rule—an insult to everyone who stresses out about making sure their bills are paid on the first of the month, or cuts back on groceries in order to cover the mortgage—it's necessary to go back to Day One of the Biden presidency, when his office issued his first executive order, "On Advancing Racial Equity and Support for Underserved Communities Through the Federal Government." In this order, Biden explained that, while "equal opportunity is the bedrock of American democracy," nevertheless "the American Dream remains out of reach" for many, owing to "entrenched disparities in our laws and public policies, and in our public and private institutions." Because of these disparities, "our Nation deserves an ambitious whole-of-government equity agenda."[2]

Issuing this executive order in the first hours of his presidency indicated the gravity, priority, and centrality of the "equity agenda" to Democrat rule. But what is that agenda? What is "equity"?

Biden's executive order began by talking about "equal opportunity," which roughly corresponds to the American ideal of equality, in the sense that most people learned about it growing up, and how we mostly think about fairness. "We hold these truths to be self-evident," wrote Thomas Jefferson in America's Declaration of Independence from England. "That all men are created equal. . . ."

Nothing better sums up the essential American credo than the idea of God-given equality. Obviously, it doesn't mean that we are all the same, equally smart, beautiful, musical, athletic, or rich. It doesn't mean that the government has to give everyone a house. What it does mean is that everybody starts from the same place of equality before God and before the law.

The idea of the equality of all people derives from natural law, a theory of morality and justice that was most profoundly articulated by Thomas Aquinas, the thirteenth-century Catholic saint and theologian. Natural law was adopted by Enlightenment thinkers, including America's founders, whose statement of separation from the English crown incorporated the principle of equal creation as a key point of contention. America, they planned, would exclude the concept of royalty, which organizes humanity into different species or castes of proximity to God.

By saying that the equality of man is "self-evident," the founders prioritized man's reason as the basis for understanding the world and society, while acknowledging that even someone of limited intellectual capacity could grasp the created equality—in the sense of value and worth in the eyes of God—of the individual human specimen.

There's no evidence—in fact, there's plenty of evidence to the contrary—that the founding premise of America was to establish a society where everyone would live equally in terms of the distribution of goods and resources. "Equality" in America has always indicated an "equality of opportunity" rather than an "equality of outcome."

In the last few years, the American Left has made a concerted effort to replace the basic idea of equality with the notion of "equity," which advocates the redistribution of resources along racial and other social lines to compensate for the unequal "starting line" for individuals that a long history of oppression has created. Probably the most influential and direct spokesperson for equity is former Vice President Kamala Harris, who released a video a few days before the 2020 election detailing the logic behind the equity agenda.

"Equality suggests, 'Oh, everyone should get the same amount,'" explained the then-junior senator from California. "The problem with that, not everybody's starting out from the same place. . . . It's about giving people the resources and the support they need so that everyone can be on equal footing and then compete on equal footing. Equitable treatment means we all end up at the same place."[3]

This is unassailable logic for first-graders and apparently maintains a deceptive clarity even for many adults—liberal clergy, talk show hosts, sociologists—who should probably know better. Yes, it would be unfair to conduct a foot race—the usual metaphor—in which some racers get a head start while some are burdened with heavy loads or forced to run in bare feet over broken glass, etc. But describing society as a predetermined contest is extraordinarily reductive and sketches a depressing vision of humanity out of *Pilgrim's Progress*.

Indeed, there is a quasi-religious, if not strictly Puritan, undercurrent to most equalitarian advocacy, based on the idea that a Heavenly City awaits us here on Earth, if only we could erase the social fictions that keep us from "all ending up at the same place." Kamala Harris's video ends with two cartoon characters—one black, one white—standing on a mountain top and basking together in the rays of the Sun of equal outcomes.

One great example of equity in action is the Covenant Homeownership Program in Washington State.[4] The program gives no-interest loans of up to $150,000 to qualified first-time homebuyers, and the loans don't have to paid back until the house is sold. Who qualifies for this program?

Based on the mandates of the Covenant Homeownership Act and the recommendations of the Covenant Homeownership Program Study, the following eligibility criteria apply:

- Household income at or below 100 percent of the Area Median Income (AMI).
- First-time homebuyer.
- The homebuyer or a parent/grandparent/great-grandparent lived in Washington state before April 1968.

April 1968 is when the federal Fair Housing Act outlawed discrimination in housing. After that point, the state of Washington acknowledges that there were still residual effects of housing discrimination, but it says that its direct responsibility for it ended there.

Here's the kicker:

- The person who lived in Washington before April 1968 is Black, Hispanic, Native American, Alaska Native, Native Hawaiian or other Pacific Islander*, Korean or Asian Indian.

---

* Following the U.S. Census definitions, "Pacific Islander" includes individuals with origins in any of the original peoples of Hawaii, Guam, Samoa, or other Pacific Islands, including, for example, Samoan, Chamorro, Tongan, Fijian, and Marshallese.

Got that? Anyone with even a distant claim to Washington State residency—a great-grandparent who was there for a few months in the 1930s—can claim $150,000 for the purchase of a house, unless they are white.

It happens to be true that the state of Washington was 96 percent white in 1968, and there probably won't be tons of people eligible to apply for the Covenant Homeownership program. But this scheme is as blatant an effort to cure the sickness with the poison that caused it as could be imagined. Chief Justice John Roberts famously wrote—in reference to a Seattle schools policy of using race as a factor in filling classroom slots—"The way to stop discrimination on the basis of race is to stop discriminating on the basis of race." Washington clearly hasn't learned this lesson, and has doubled down on its use of racism to stop racism.

The chief theorist of the philosophy of equity today is Ibram X. Kendi, a writer born to a middle-class black family in the borough of Queens in New York City—one of the few counties in the United States where, as recently as 2005, the black household median income exceeded that of non-Hispanic white households. Kendi's parents were professionals and sent him to private schools through junior high. They moved to Virginia, where he went to a nice suburban public school.

Kendi became internationally famous and a bestselling author for popularizing Critical Race Theory and his conception of "antiracism." As Kendi lays out in his book *How to Be an Antiracist*, white racism is the defining context of modern American life. It is so pervasive that we don't even see it. White people in particular are blind to it. Kendi, who was given tens of millions of dollars a few months after the George Floyd riots of 2020 to found the Center for Antiracist Research at Boston University—which went broke and closed its doors within five years—says that "there's no such thing as 'not racist.'"

That is, the normal, commonsense understanding of not being racist by treating other people as individuals rather than as members of a group is insufficiently nonracist. In fact, according to Kendi, "the concept of 'not-racism' is really just an act of denial." Calling yourself a "nonracist" is a form of racism. And since most people usually deny they are racist, and avowed racists are hard to find these days, nonracism is the most prevalent form of racism.

Liberals and conservatives alike are fond of quoting Martin Luther King Jr. and his professed dream of a future where his children "will one day live in a nation where they will not be judged by the color of their skin, but by the content of their character." This is the sort of sentiment—proclaimed in 1963, when segregation and discrimination on the basis of race in hiring, housing, and public accommodations was still legal in many states—that softened up America for the advent of civil rights and the institutionalization of a new regime that would supersede the U.S. Constitution, install judges as the effective rulers of the land, and transform the nation into something unrecognizably different.[5]

And why shouldn't it have? King's vision, asking just that his children be judged as *specific* individuals—as specimens, or members of the human species—rather than as inhabitants of a range on the spectrum of melanin content, addresses the ideal of equality before God and law that the Founders inscribed into the charter documents of the nation. To judge someone by their "character" means, in the fullest sense, to evaluate them by their words and deeds. "Character" indicates reputation, conduct, moral qualities, and habits. Its original meaning referred to engraving or stamping, and in this sense a person's character is ingrained and, it is vital to stress, *legible*. The individual black person, in King's idealized expression, would engage with the republic like everyone else, naked except for what they brought to the table as a human subject in commerce and dialogue with others.

King's dream, then, called for a fulfillment of the Jeffersonian principle of equality and its extension to the black population, as American society had slowly opened the franchise to include nonpropertied white men, women, and Indians. Americans under the age of 60 or so grew up with a sense of Martin Luther King Jr. as a combination saint, martyr, philosopher, and savior. His picture hung in classrooms, his birthday is commemorated as a national holiday—he is the only American accorded this honor. (Technically, George Washington's birthday is observed at the federal level, but in common practice and most states it has become President's Day.)

So, why is it that quoting King on judging people not by the color of their skin but the content of their character has become so corny, so retrograde, that leading-edge experts on racism will roll their eyes when they hear it? Every January, we are treated to explanations about how King's words are "misused," "distorted," "weaponized," and "misappropriated" by conservatives who are eager to make him sound like he believed what he said.

Ronald Reagan opposed the passage of the Civil Rights Act in 1964, but two decades later, as president, he signed legislation establishing Martin Luther King Jr. Day as a federal holiday. Though Reagan explained that he thought King's memory would be better celebrated as an unofficial holiday, he said he would go along with the consensus that the man deserved significant commemoration.

At the Rose Garden bill-signing ceremony, Reagan spoke without reservation about King's legacy, reminding the audience that the Montgomery bus boycott—organized and led by King—had "stunned the country" and resulted in federal courts declaring that segregation in public transportation violated the Equal Protection Clause of the 14th Amendment to the Constitution. Reagan continued, proclaiming that "King had awakened something strong and true, a sense that true justice must be colorblind, and that among white and black Americans, as he put it, 'Their destiny is tied up with our destiny, and their freedom is inextricably bound to our freedom; we cannot walk alone.'"[6]

The insistence on the colorblind essence of King's message drives the Left crazy, because the Left is dedicated—as much as any hardcore white supremacist—to the idea that skin color is the defining element of morality, society, and human worth. Any value system that doesn't prioritize racial identity, according to this ideology, lives in denial of the racism that shoots through the structure of society from top to bottom.

The most prominent antiracist theorist in America—at least the most prominent white one—is Robin DiAngelo, whose book *White Fragility* became practically a subindustry in the massive Diversity, Equity, and Inclusion enterprise. The book came out in 2018 and hit the bestseller list, but it really took off after the George Floyd riots in the Summer of 2020. Anxious white liberals, desperate to put a name to their mixed feelings of guilt and superiority to the deplorable white masses, harkened to DiAngelo's message, which defined "white fragility" as "an expectation of racial comfort" and a "lack of racial stamina."

According to DiAngelo, white people swim in white supremacy so effortlessly and enjoy their unearned privilege so thoroughly that "even a minimal challenge to the white position becomes intolerable." The "fragility" she assigns to whites manifests itself in "argumentation, invalidation, silence, withdrawal and claims of being attacked and misunderstood." These illegitimate responses—none of which, by the way, sounds especially dangerous—"reinstate white racial equilibrium and maintain control."

Robin DiAngelo details how Martin Luther King Jr.'s message has been expropriated as a slogan of white supremacy, a perfect example of "racism's ability to adapt to cultural changes." Racism, she means us to understand, is so pernicious and slippery that it can transmute even the words of our nation's patron saint of racial equality into Nazi propaganda, which is essentially how DiAngelo casts the idea of colorblindness. Not able to bring herself to quote King directly, DiAngelo refers to it as "a line from the famous 'I Have a Dream' speech."

DiAngelo writes:

> One line of King's speech in particular—that one day he might be judged by the content of his character and not the color of his skin—was seized upon by the white public because the words were seen to provide a simple and immediate solution to racial tensions: pretend that we don't see race, and racism will end. Color blindness was now promoted as the remedy for racism, with white people insisting that they didn't see race or, if they did, that it had no meaning to them . . . reducing King's work **to this simplistic idea** illustrates how movements for social change are co-opted, stripped of their initial challenge, and used against the very cause from which they originated. [emphasis added][7]

Calling King's most famous and affecting sentiment—that people should be judged by the content of their character rather than the color of their skin—a "simplistic idea" that perverts the real meaning of King's philosophy is a fantastic inversion of reality. DiAngelo is doing exactly what she accuses her enemies of doing, using King's words "against the very cause from which they originated." In a similar vein, in a 2017 *Boston Review* article called "Reagan Used MLK Day to Undermine Racial Justice," authors Christopher Petrella and Justin Gomer—a couple of white up-and-comers in the world of antiracist scholarship—explain that "Reagan's frequent citation of King marked the beatification of King not as a champion of racial justice but of colorblind ideology." According to Petrella and Gomer, Reagan "thought little of King, ultimately used the creation of a national holiday honoring King as a way to co-opt his legacy, enabling Reagan ironically to oppose key civil rights laws in the name of aligning himself with King's supposedly colorblind dream."

Yet, all of these theorists acknowledge that overt racism, of the sort that motivated the civil rights movement, is a little scarce these days. Racially motivated violence certainly occurs, though on balance it mostly goes the other way, with black perpetrators committing a disproportionate amount of interracial crime. And white-on-black hate crimes, such as the 1998 dragging death of James Byrd, are typically punished swiftly and surely—two of Byrd's killers were executed, and the third will spend his life in prison. Legally speaking, there is no "systemic racism" in America if by "systemic" we mean officially sanctioned or permitted discrimination against nonwhites. Activists like Ibram X. Kendi insist that any racial disparity in American society is definitive evidence of racism, but so far as overt institutional racism goes, it is long gone.

But, as Kendi, DiAngelo, and the rest of the massive DEI superstructure explain, America is just as racist as ever, even if vanishingly few people are openly racist. *Racism Without Racists*, a 2003 book by noted sociologist and Duke University superstar Eduardo Bonilla-Silva, describes the new prevailing construct. Overtly crude racism, of the sort demonstrated by louts pouring milkshakes over the heads of segregated lunch counter protestors, or blowing up black churches with impunity, is socially and professionally unacceptable. In its place, we are told, racism has refined itself and become as vaporous as the air we breathe—and just as ubiquitous and essential to white supremacy.

For instance, the University of California at Santa Cruz—academic home of Angela Davis—produced a handout on "microaggressions," which it defines as "the everyday verbal, nonverbal, and environmental slights, snubs, or insults, whether intentional or unintentional, that communicate hostile, derogatory, or negative messages to target persons based solely upon their marginalized group membership."[8]

The idea of microaggressivity is that overt racism has become socially and legally unacceptable, so it has gone underground and now takes the form of slights so minor as to be practically imperceptible. Of course, this is the same as saying that, because racist *macroaggressions* like lynchings or race riots have disappeared from American society, it is necessary for race-obsessed ideologues to swap in a new and more powerful lens to their instruments, in order to discern tiny disturbances to racial harmony.

So, a woman who "clutches her purse" when a black person walks by is guilty of a microaggression, according to the University of California—except, properly speaking, it is a woman who is simply *perceived* by a black person to have clutched her purse who is guilty. She may have only been adjusting her gait or looking for a stick of gum.

Microaggressions are subjective and personal. There is no way to track or quantify them, unlike racial violence or actual discrimination that takes the form of salary or performance evaluation. Sensitivity to microaggressions encourages everyone to become neurotic and paranoid and is part of the same feminization of society and the workplace that has elevated human resource departments and their diversity commissars to the highest levels of the corporate executive suite.

The University of California handout on microaggressions names "Color Blindness" as a major theme for covert racism, describing it as "Statements that indicate that a White person does not want to or need to acknowledge race." Offending state-ments include such anodyne, familiar mottoes as "There is only one race, the human race," or "I don't believe in race," or "All lives matter." Someone who speaks this way, the handout explains, is "Denying the significance of a person of color's racial/ethnic experience and history."

Of course, it's not an extreme statement to note that the apo-thegm "There is only one race, the human race" is the essential lesson of all American education, the maxim that is ground into our consciousness across all media from the instant we begin to understand speech. The *New York Times*, NPR, *The Atlantic* magazine, all network and cable television, ministers and rabbis, scientists . . . all tell us, all the time, that "race does not exist" and that the differences within races are far more significant than the differences among races.

Jane Elliott is an antiracism educator, now in her nineties, who became famous for conducting an apartheid-style exercise in her third-grade classroom the day after MLK's assassination. She split the class up between kids with blue eyes and kids with brown eyes and treated one group (the blue-eyed kids) harshly and told the other group that they were allowed and expected to treat their blue-eyed classmates as inferiors. This exercise, which caught on and gave Jane Elliott a long and lucrative career enact-ing this program for church groups, corporate diversity retreats, and teacher enrichment training sessions, demonstrated the arbi-trary and cruel nature of racial segregation.

Yet, even Jane Elliott, who has been pursuing the anti-racist agenda with a vengeance for more than a half a century, declares "One Race" to be her core teaching. "Just stop believing that there's more than one race," she told the *New York Times* in 2020. "Realize that we're all members of the same race. That's the human race."[9]

So, why is saying that we are all one human race a micro-aggression, if it's also an essential truth of America in the Civil Rights Era? For the same reason that it's appropriate for some people to celebrate Martin Luther King Day and an exercise in depraved cynicism when other people do it. The Left is willing to accept the fact that King referred to the colorblind ideal in his famous 1963 speech. What they find disgusting is the fact that conservatives cite it as evidence that King was, even to the slightest extent, on their side.

The point of all this is simply to demonstrate how the meaning of the word "racist" has shifted. A racist used to be someone who wanted to treat different people differently; today, a racist is someone who wants to treat different people the same. Or, a racist used to be someone who didn't like nonwhites; today, a racist is anyone nonwhites don't like.

So, when leftists talk about "equity," we see what's at stake. They aren't talking about political equality or any of the freedoms and rights that Americans are entitled to—that's old thinking, based around the principle of equality, which means "equal opportunity." Equity means "equality of outcome." And when we are talking about outcomes, we are talking about *stuff*. Steve Sailer, an incisive commentator on matters of race and culture in America, quips that when people talk about achieving equity, what they mean is your *home equity*, which they plan to absorb.

This section of the book will examine the ways in which the Left wages war against local communities by weaponizing the history of race relations, residential segregation, and climate change in order to destabilize suburban neighborhoods through radical densification and the transformation of transportation infrastructure.

It is now an accepted premise on the Left that residential segregation reinforced and solidified racial inequality in America, specifically by enabling white people to accrue significant wealth—"generational wealth"—through homeownership. Specific policies, carried out since the 1930s, have encouraged whites to buy houses while relegating nonwhites, especially blacks, to being tenants. Trillions of dollars of home equity accrued to white households, while black people poured their money into rents that added up, in the long run, to nothing.

This narrative begins with the New Deal and Franklin Roosevelt's massive expansion of the federal government to pull the United States out of the Depression. Whether or not the New Deal succeeded in this task, or whether it in fact prolonged the Depression, is a question that historians and economists will bicker over, but there is no question that the New Deal transformed the nation. When FDR took over as president, the amount the federal government spent as a share of the total economy was around 5 percent; today it is roughly 25 percent. The omnipresent nature of the federal state in American life today, oriented around entitlement spending, an imperial foreign outlook, and massive tax collection, was largely instituted by Roosevelt and the New Deal.

One key New Deal program—and the purported cause of persistent racial inequality up to the present moment—was federal mortgage insurance. A series of bank failures starting in 1930 severely constricted America's money supply and the availability of credit. In 1933, the federal government began to encourage banks to lend money to aspiring homeowners by guaranteeing the underlying debt. The Home Owners' Loan Corporation (HOLC) bought existing mortgage loans, refinanced them, and then serviced the loans; the Federal Housing Administration (FHA), beginning in 1934, insured new mortgages, aiming to increase homebuying among lower- and middle-income people. The FHA, in particular, established the 20 percent down, 30-year term length that became standard across the mortgage lending industry.

"Redlining" came into play around this time. The term refers to neighborhood maps created by the HOLC that identified areas as more or less suitable to lenders. The maps, and accompanying notes, looked at the quality and age of neighborhood housing stock, the history and trends of sales, and the percentage of buildings that were multifamily dwellings. They considered neighborhood proximity to amenities such as parks and transit, or to less-favorable features like prisons and garbage dumps. They considered the demographic composition of the neighborhood, including average salary, the percentage of foreign-born people, the dominant ethnicities in the area, and whether there was a substantial "Negro" presence. Based on these factors, neighborhoods would be evaluated as either a good, fair, or poor credit risk for lenders. The areas considered least suitable for mortgage insurance were colored red and hence were "redlined."

Redlining has come to mean the deliberate denial of mortgages to people living in black neighborhoods, and the restriction of black people to neighborhoods colored red on the HOLC maps. But beyond this, it has become a heuristic—a convenient mental shorthand—for the Left to explain why black Americans, on average, have less wealth than white people. It is no exaggeration to say that, in the last few decades, redlining has become the standard answer to the question of why blacks seem to have been left behind in American society, despite the end of legal segregation. Anywhere you turn, redlining is cited as the mechanism and engine of inequality.

Richard Rothstein is the author of *The Color of Law: A Forgotten History of How Our Government Segregated America*, which came out in 2017 and quickly changed the discourse about how people in the know talk about race relations. While books like *White Fragility* or *How to Be an Antiracist* advanced arguments about systemic racism that were compelling to a certain uninformed readership impressed by the idea—akin to astrology or "the law of attraction"—that unseen magical forces like "implicit racism" compel us to behave unconsciously, the thesis of *The Color of Law* is backed by data and historical analysis that academics and intellectual types could take seriously. Rothstein argues in *The Color of Law* that:

> ... until the last quarter of the twentieth century, racially explicit policies of federal, state, and local governments defined where whites and African Americans should live. Today's residential segregation in the North, South, Midwest, and West is not the unintended consequence of individual choices and of otherwise well-meaning law or regulation but of unhidden public policy that explicitly segregated every metropolitan area in the United States. The policy was so systematic and forceful that its effects endure to the present time. Without our government's purposeful imposition of racial segregation, the other causes—private prejudice, white flight, real estate steering, bank redlining, income differences, and self-segregation— still would have existed but with far less opportunity for expression. Segregation by intentional government action is not de facto. Rather, it is what courts call de jure: segregation by law and public policy.

Redlining, along with other government-supported policies such as slum clearance ("urban renewal"), the allocation of public housing units, and the construction of the interstate highway system are central to Rothstein's argument about racial segregation in America. The book received rave reviews from national media. The *New York Times* put it on its bestseller list for 32 weeks (the *Times* bestseller list, it should be noted, reflects editorial decisions and is not a statistically driven count of the books that were actually sold in the previous week), and said of *The Color of Law* that there was "no better history" of housing segregation. Bill Gates listed it as one of his "Amazing Books" of the year. And Pete Buttigieg, Biden's Secretary of Transportation, called it a "really important book" and suggested that "it would make sense if resources went into creating that racial inequity that resources would go into reversing it."[10]

The supposed effects of redlining have been immense—in fact, unimaginably so. They have, according to the antiracist Left, been central to the formation of the "wealth gap" that starkly divides black and white America. As the Federal Reserve Bank of Minneapolis indicates, "The racial wealth gap is the largest of the economic disparities between Black and white Americans, with a white-to-Black per capita wealth ratio of 6 to 1."[11] It is also "among the most persistent." Indeed, according to the Federal Reserve Board, in 2016 the median white family had a net worth of $171,000, versus the median black family's net worth of just $17,600. There is also a discrepancy between whites and blacks in regard to income, though it is not nearly so wide as the wealth gap.

The Left has embraced the idea of "generational wealth" as something that whites have been encouraged to build while blacks have been systematically stymied from accruing it. More specifically, according to the prevailing narrative, whites were encouraged to buy homes, both in the suburbs and the nicer areas of cities, which allowed them to generate astounding levels of unearned wealth. Blacks, on the other hand, were shunted into substandard housing for which they were forced to pay a premium.

"The suburbs were invented as a reactionary tool against the women's liberation and civil rights movements," *The Nation* reports in a 2023 article called "America's Suburbs Are Breeding Grounds for Fascism."[12] Author P. E. Moskowitz continues, explaining that "the U.S. government, in concert with banks, landowners, and home builders, created a way to try and stop all that, by separating people into single homes, removing public spaces, and ensuring that every neighborhood was segregated via redlining. The suburbs would keep white women at home, and would keep white men at work to afford that home."

This dystopian fantasy of suburban sterility is nothing new, of course, and given its staggering unoriginality one wonders if Moskowitz is even aware of the long history of suburbia-mocking that preceded it. Starting from Sinclair Lewis's 1922 *Babbitt* through Richard Yates's 1962 *Revolutionary Road* and Don DeLillo's 1985 *White Noise*—not to mention movies like *American Beauty*, *Ordinary People*, and *The Ice Storm*—American literature has thoroughly excavated the mine of materialism, sexual hypocrisy, small-mindedness, emotional constipation, and barely contained racial savagery that is supposed to characterize the savage sterility of suburban life.

Folk singer Malvina Reynolds's 1962 "Little Boxes," amplified by Communist folk hero Pete Seeger into a minor hit on the hootenany circuit, remains probably the best example of self-righteous leftist disgust for suburban neighborhoods and the bourgeois sensibility its architecture embodies.

> Little boxes on the hillside
> Little boxes made of ticky tacky
> Little boxes on the hillside
> Little boxes all the same

There's a pink one and a green one
And a blue one and a yellow one
And they're all made out of ticky tacky
And they all look just the same

And the people in the houses
All went to the university
Where they were put in boxes
And they came out all the same

The souls of suburban folk, it is understood, are trimmed to fit the anonymized and anodyne terrain of the suburban landscape. Nothing unusual or special can grow there. The little boxes replicate themselves and turn out new versions of their talentless inhabitants in a nightmarish, sterile vision.

A potted history of the suburbs—the received narrative that can be found virtually everywhere you look—is offered to us by the venerable National Low Income Housing Coalition:

> Whites fled cities to move to outlying majority white middle-class enclaves in the mid-1900s, a phenomenon known as "white flight." The federal government encouraged whites to move to suburbs by constructing federal highways and providing white families low-interest mortgages for homes in car-centric, less dense neighborhoods. Racist residential segregation policies, like redlining, housing discrimination, and racially restrictive covenants, limited opportunities for people of color to follow the same path.[13]

The "phenomenon known as 'white flight'" is an important nemesis in standard histories of American urban policy. During

World War I, blacks began moving to Northern cities in a mass movement of people that continued until the early 1970s. The "Great Migration" had several waves, before and after the Depression, and saw approximately seven million African Americans leave the South, driven by racial repression and lured by the promise of work in the booming industrial economy of the North.

The rapid urbanization of what had been a largely rural population was tremendously dislocating, both for the black Southerners and the Northern cities that absorbed them. As late as 1940, New York City was about 95 percent non-Hispanic white, and neighborhoods that are today considered entirely and historically nonwhite—including East Harlem in Manhattan, the Tremont area of the Bronx, and Brownsville and East New York in Brooklyn—were largely Jewish and Italian districts into the 1950s and 1960s.

The movement of blacks and Puerto Ricans into traditionally white urban areas, and the departure of many of the legacy residents for the suburbs, is called "white flight" because the white population is understood to have "fled" in a terrified evacuation driven by racist preoccupations about safety and real estate values. Unscrupulous real estate agents practiced "blockbusting" by stealthily permitting occasional black families to buy homes in white neighborhoods, and then sowed fear in the surrounding community that housing prices were about to collapse. Nervous white homeowners would, in panic, sell into a falling market, enabling the unscrupulous agents to buy whole neighborhoods for a pittance, and then sell them at a premium to black buyers desperate for homes.

Former First Lady Michelle Obama relates the history of South Shore in Chicago, her hometown and neighborhood of origin, in just these terms, explaining how white families abandoned the area because of "the color of our skin" and "the texture of our hair."[14] She explains that whites "were afraid of what our families represented" and ran from the South Side of Chicago out of fear, not as a result of rational planning or the search for a "better life." *New York Times* columnist Jamelle Bouie, responding in 2011 to the idea that rising crime rates may have contributed to "white flight," notes that "the largest influx of whites from urban centers and to the suburbs—including Detroit—predated the crime explosion of the 1970s and '80s by at least a decade."[15]

It's true that crime rates exploded in the 1970s and '80s, though it is somewhat disingenuous of Bouie to pretend that Detroit hadn't been affected by racial tension before that time. The Detroit riot of 1967 was the bloodiest and most destructive riot in the United States since the New York draft riots in 1863, resulting in 43 deaths and 400 burned-out buildings. Throughout the '60s, the rates of property and violent crime in Detroit more than doubled.

The story is the same in cities across the industrial heartland, from St. Louis and Cleveland to Detroit and Chicago, and from Newark and New York to Baltimore and Philadelphia—as blacks moved to the cities, crime went up, and whites left. As William Voegeli perceptively notes concerning Michelle Obama's beloved home, "During the two decades that South Shore changed from a white neighborhood to a black one, it also changed from a safe neighborhood to a dangerous one. Over the four decades since it became overwhelmingly black, it has remained dangerous."[16]

Neoconservative writer Norman Podhoretz famously and controversially addressed the question of black urban crime and the white experience of it in a 1963 article called "My Negro Problem—and Ours." Published in *Commentary*, Podhoretz reflected on his childhood in the Brownsville section of Brooklyn in the 1930s. He discusses being torn between what he read in the papers and heard from authoritative figures, and the "evidence of my own senses," regarding the twinned notions that "all Jews were rich" and "all Negroes were persecuted."

Podhoretz's article infuriates people to this day for its blunt discussion of race relations among the urban poor during the Depression. "For a long time," he wrote, "I was puzzled to think that Jews were supposed to be rich when the only Jews I knew were poor, and that Negroes were supposed to be persecuted when it was the Negroes who were doing the only persecuting I knew about—and doing it, moreover, to me."[17]

Jewish leftists in particular return to this 60-year-old article in outrage. Though everyone knows that the statistical reality of interracial crime is overwhelmingly black-on-everyone-else, we are asked, nay ordered, against the evidence of our own senses, to go along with the story that black people suffer, not just economic or residential grief, but actual physical persecution at the hands of white people. Mentioning the facts about who perpetrates violent crime against whom is a kind of "malinformation," to use a neologism of the Biden years: It may be true, but it can be used maliciously, and therefore it is worse than a lie, which, after all, can be disproven.

In any event, it is nonsensical to argue that white flight was strictly a question of racist whites not wanting to be near black people, no matter what Michelle Obama ("I want to remind white folks that y'all were running from us") says. Part of the white migration to the suburbs was a matter of rising crime and the decay of public order. And part of it was a desire to pursue the American Dream of having a detached house, a yard, fresh air, and more space to raise a family.

White flight, according to the same narrative, was lubricated by the construction of the interstate highway system, which viciously cut through downtowns and opened a path for aspiring suburbanites to flee. Expressways, built largely after World War

II, "made suburban housing available on one end while destroying urban housing on the other," explains urbanist Kevin Kuswa. Deborah Archer, an NYU law professor, president of the American Civil Liberties Union, and the national authority on how "highway construction displaced Black households and cut the heart and soul out of thriving Black communities as homes, churches, schools, and businesses were destroyed," describes in her famous essay "White Men's Roads Through Black Men's Homes," the "legacy of highway politics that focus on growth and expansion at the expense of Black communities: by building roads to whites-only suburbs through the heart of Black neighborhoods."[18]

It is virtually a given now that the expansion of the highway system included a wide effort to destabilize black communities and keep black Americans impoverished. In 2021, Bloomberg produced a lavish set of maps demonstrating how highways through major cities in many cases went through predominantly African American neighborhoods. "Take any major American city and you're likely to find a historically Black neighborhood demolished, gashed in two, or cut off from the rest of the city by a highway," Bloomberg explained. "This legacy of racist federal transportation policies continues to define the landscapes of urban spaces."[19]

There is a certain truth to this story. Highways in many major cities did cut through black neighborhoods. But they also cut through other neighborhoods. Expressways aren't waste transfer stations, bus depots, or prisons, or the type of discrete negative feature that critics claim are frequently located in politically weak communities. Highways stretch for miles and connect distant locations. The point of the expressway system was to provide rapid and easy access into city centers; necessarily, certain downtown neighborhoods were going to be disrupted.

Probably the most famous example of a neighborhood that was destroyed by a highway is the working-class East Tremont section of the Bronx, through which Robert Moses slammed the Cross Bronx Expressway beginning in 1949, displacing several thousand families with brutal efficiency. Robert Caro's famous book *The Power Broker* vividly describes how the local community was devastated, and Caro makes a compelling argument that the Cross Bronx Expressway essentially set the stage for the socioeconomic collapse of the South Bronx in decades to come.

The grim consequences were so stark that their effects are being felt to this day, according to critics. Robert Moses "became a leading advocate for displacing Black communities to build the highway system, and his ideas were widely adopted around the country," explains Deborah Archer. "The Cross Bronx Expressway, built by Robert Moses, is both literally and metaphorically a structure of racism," inveighs Bronx Congressman Ritchie Torres. The Institute for Transportation and Development Policy, an influential leftist group, calls the Cross Bronx Expressway an "often cited example of how highways have decimated communities of color." Former Democrat candidate for president Andrew Yang said it's "an egregious example of how urban planners, like Robert Moses, built highways without regard for existing communities of color and tore apart neighborhoods."

Deborah Archer cites a tendentious and common critique of Robert Moses: that he intentionally built parkway bridges low to prevent buses from riding on the roads.

He took great pains to build New York's roads and highways in a way that would limit the ability of poor people of color to visit the parks and beaches he built. For example, Moses instructed highway engineers to build the bridges across the Southern State Parkway with one foot less clearance than bridges on the Hutchinson, Saw Mill, and Bronx River Parkways. The clearance was intentionally too low for buses coming from New York City to pass, as he believed Black and Puerto Rican New Yorkers would most likely use buses to access the beach. As a result, bus trips to the beach would have to be made on local roads, making the trips "discouragingly long and arduous." The law already prohibited commercial traffic, including trucks and buses, from using all the American parkways. When asked why he made the bridges low, Moses replied, "Legislation can always be changed; It's very hard to tear down a bridge once it's up."

Sounds pretty bad. But construction on the Southern State Parkway began in 1925 in order to improve access to Jones Beach. Census data of that period indicates that New York City was 97 percent white. Only 2 percent of the city was black. And though the Puerto Rican population of the city did rise significantly in the 1920s, by 1930 there were about 45,000 Puerto Ricans in New York, or less than 1 percent of the total population.

So, even if Robert Moses designed the route to Jones Beach to prevent buses from getting there, it wasn't racially motivated, because there weren't enough minorities in New York City to make this workable. In any case, there has always been public transportation, including buses, to Jones Beach.

The low-clearance parkway bridges and the demolition of the South Bronx to create the Cross Bronx Expressway are seen as classic representations of the power of racism to instantiate itself into the racial geography of the built environment. The story is so juicy and teachable it makes one's knees weak. But the core problem with this narrative is that no "communities of color" were disrupted by the construction of the Cross Bronx Expressway. The East Tremont neighborhood was almost entirely Jewish. It is true that the neighborhood later came to be inhabited mostly by blacks and Puerto Ricans, but the idea, as former secretary of transportation Pete Buttigieg put it, that racism is "built into" the highway system is tendentious, as is his claim that highways were often "built for the purpose of dividing a white and a black neighborhood."

Buttigieg here makes a curious turn, one that we hear frequently. Sometimes, we are told, highways were built through black neighborhoods, as in the Black Bottom section of Detroit. This is offered as an example of how the highway system destroyed cohesive, vibrant black neighborhoods. Sometimes they were built between black and white neighborhoods, as in the case of Chicago's South Side. This is an example of how highways imposed and deepened racial segregation. There are also many poor black neighborhoods that are nowhere near a highway— were they excluded from participation in the economy and thus doomed to social isolation?

The critics have set up a "heads they win, tails you lose" argument regarding expressways and racism. It is true that many highways went through black neighborhoods in inner cities, but the Federal-Aid Highway Act of 1956 provided billions of dollars for the construction of 41,000 miles of new roads. Many highways were built through white communities, too. Corktown is a historically white neighborhood in Detroit that was largely plowed under in the late 1950s to make way for I-75; some 400 businesses and residences were razed. Frog Hollow in Hartford, Connecticut, was a dense Irish and Italian neighborhood that was divided by the construction of I-84 in the '60s.

The post-war period in America was a moment of astonishing prosperity and growth. The automobile was central to any mainstream vision of the American future. The Highway Act of 1956 passed Congress with near unanimity. Among public intellectuals, there was little criticism of the centrality of the car and the necessity of building highways to accommodate travel. One exception was philosopher of technology, literary critic, and urban theorist Lewis Mumford, whose ideal city was essentially a fourteenth-century English market town. But most were enthusiastic. Automobile ownership grew steadily after the war ended; in 1950, there were more cars than households for the first time. As Tom Lewis notes in his 1997 book *Divided Highways*, motorists, truckers, mayors, and contractors were all "ecstatic" about the Act:

> No doubt the happiest groups of all were the manufacturers of automobiles and trucks and the refiners of gasoline. More and better roads promised a steady increase in the number of miles motor vehicles traveled. Seventy-two percent of American families owned an automobile in 1956. By 1970, the number had risen to eighty-two percent; and twenty-eight percent owned two or more automobiles. In the same period, personal purchases of gasoline and automobiles more than doubled. Congress had voted to enact nothing less than a fundamental change in American life. Nearly all acclaimed the decision.[20]

America did not need to be tricked into building a national highway system, nor was racism on the list of things the highways were supposed to accomplish. Is it really surprising that politically weak communities—black and white—were least empowered to prevent powerful forces of development from impinging on their infrastructure?

Is it credible to imagine that highways were designed primarily to destroy black neighborhoods, or did black communities, politically weak and, in some cases, inhabiting convenient locations for interchanges and cloverleafs, have to deal with the same upheaval that affected hundreds of thousands, if not millions, of Americans at the same time?

In any event, the post-war move to the suburbs is described by the Left as a kind of elaborate plot in which blacks were lured North, set to work in the dark, satanic mills until industry collapsed, and then abandoned to live in rotting ghettoes as the white former residents ran off with their lucre. It is literally interpreted as a form of theft. The Brookings Institution is the nation's most venerable policy center, highly respected and influential in elite centers of power. A recent Brookings report explains that "homes in predominately Black neighborhoods across the country are valued at $48,000 less than predominately white neighborhoods for a cumulative loss in equity of approximately $156 billion. These are significant contributing factors to the racial wealth gap."

It's no doubt true—and virtually axiomatic—that predominantly black neighborhoods have cheaper homes than predominantly white neighborhoods. We will address the question of home valuation and appraisal in the next section, but note that Brookings explains this difference as a "cumulative loss in equity." If my house is worth less than your house, you may have more equity than I do, but it's hardly fair to say that I have "lost" equity or that you gained it at my expense.

But the authors at Brookings follow this up with a doozy:

Lower Black homeownership and the racial wealth
gap are byproducts of systemic racism, including the
legacies of slavery, Jim Crow segregation, redlining,
and other anti-Black policies that targeted Black people

and predominately Black neighborhoods. **Residential segregation facilitates the extraction of wealth and other vital resources** that fuel economic and social mobility. The loss of wealth in Black communities hastens a downward socioeconomic spiral. [emphasis added][21]

It's not just that black people have less wealth than white people, but white wealth has been "extracted" (read: stolen) from black people through the process of residential segregation. The mechanism of action for how this works is not explained. It is merely presupposed that the relation of whites and blacks in America is parallel to a classic colonial relation, where the colony is subject to enforced economic underdevelopment to promote the development of the mother country.

It's embarrassing—or should be, anyway—that the Brookings Institution would employ such vulgar logic in an important policy report. But this is the kind of illogic that passes for sociological rigor in analyses of race in America today. One of Ibram X. Kendi's most famous arguments, in support of a proposed "anti-racist amendment to the Constitution," is that "racial inequity is evidence of racist policy." That is, any difference in outcome ("racial inequity") is necessarily and presumptively evidence of racism.

This formulation is not so far off from where we already are. New York City recently agreed that the failure rate of black people who took the test to be a teacher in the public schools was high enough that it was evidence that the test was racially biased against black test takers. Some people asked to see the racist questions, but the point was lost on them: The particular questions weren't racist, the *test* was racist, because a higher percentage of black people than other races didn't pass it. Plenty of black people did pass it, of course, but that's also beside the point. New

York agreed to pay back salary, including imputed raises and bonuses and pension contributions, to dozens of black people who couldn't pass the teacher test, in some cases decades ago.

This isn't especially unusual. American judges have routinely used the logic of "disparate impact" to make sweeping determinations about a range of social phenomena. In fact, Kendi's suggested constitutional amendment would almost be redundant, because disparate impact is already an important element of federal law when it comes to determining employment discrimination. The appearance of disparate outcomes in facially neutral hiring and advancement creates a rebuttable presumption of racial prejudice on the part of the employer and requires the employer to prove that the outcomes reflect a job-related business necessity.

You may recall during the pandemic—when all leftists suddenly became experts on virology and epidemiology—hearing people lecture us that "correlation does not imply causation." This maxim means that it's not enough just to point from A to B and assume a direct line connects them—you need to offer proof of cause and effect. But when it comes to questions of racial inequity, correlation always implies—or proves—causation.

Wealth extraction is a popular way for leftists to explain inequality. As former President Barack Obama famously said, "You didn't build that." Or as socialist Congresswoman Alexandria Ocasio-Cortez likes to say, "No one ever makes a billion dollars. You take a billion dollars." Of course, you could say the same thing about a million dollars. Or a thousand dollars. Why should you have a hundred dollars when someone else has only one dollar? The idea that anyone creates wealth through industry or ingenuity is a lie, according to this perspective, because all wealth really derives, ultimately, from society. The job of government is to reorganize wealth and return it to its proper place. Bill de

Blasio, the former mayor of New York City, summed up this argument neatly when he announced, "There's plenty of money in this town, it's just in the wrong hands."[22]

So, the idea that (white) people in the suburbs extract wealth from (black) people in the cities makes perfect sense if you figure that white people living in suburbs work in cities, where black people live. The whites commute into the city, extract the money, and go home.

If you want a better explanation than that, I challenge you to find one. You won't find it from the Brookings Institution. This isn't to say that there is no wealth inequality in America. But to say that it's all "extracted" from black people is tendentious and false.

The Center for American Progress (CAP)—a major Washington policy and advocacy center closely tied to the Democratic Party—notes that "the iterative nature of wealth begetting more wealth means that without public interventions, it will be virtually impossible for Black Americans to catch up to their white counterparts." Referring to the "iterative nature of wealth," CAP gestures to the notion that money attracts money, building in families from generation to generation. Wealth "begets" itself in a natural process, and white people pass on ever-growing gardens of abundance to their children and grandchildren.[23]

Indeed, the question of inheritance is raised frequently in this discourse of equity. The Economic Policy Institute (EPI), a left-wing think tank and advocacy group with ties to the Democratic Party, and the employer of Richard Rothstein, explains that "white families are twice as likely to receive an inheritance as black families, and that inheritance is nearly three times as much."[24] Supreme Court Justice Ketanji Brown Jackson, in her 2023 dissent to the Court's ruling that race-based affirmative action programs in higher education are generally unconstitutional, began her 53-page opinion by noting, "Gulf-sized race-based gaps exist with respect to the health, wealth, and well-being of American citizens. They were created in the distant past, but have indisputably been passed down to the present day through the generations."[25]

Referencing the color-coded HOLC maps and the redlining that blocked blacks from accruing generational wealth from homeownership, Justice Jackson added that "it is significant that, in so excluding Black people, government policies affirmatively operated—one could say, affirmatively acted—to dole out preferences to those who, if nothing else, were not Black. Those past preferences carried forward and are reinforced today by (among other things) the benefits that flow to homeowners and to the holders of other forms of capital that are hard to obtain unless one already has assets."

But how true to life is this picture of white generational wealth? The EPI study referenced above notes that whites are more likely to receive an inheritance than black families, but a closer look at the data is revealing. As it happens, only 20 percent of the population inherits anything at all. Don't forget, the bottom 90 percent of the country controls only 31 percent of the wealth, and the bottom 50 percent only has one-fortieth of the pie. White people are still a majority of the country, and you can expect to find plenty of them in the lower depths, too. Most people, of whatever race, live and die without accruing much in the way of wealth except knickknacks.

The median inheritance among white people is about $15,000, which is indeed larger than the median black inheritance of around $3,000, but it's like a distinction without a difference—it amounts to a more elaborate headstone, when you get down to it.[26]

So, what happens to all that iterative, generational wealth? Well, dying is expensive. It used to be that few people lived to be 80; these days, being 90 or 95 is nothing special. About 7 percent of all people over 65—a growing segment of the population—live

in nursing homes or assisted living facilities, and that proportion grows steadily as people age. Long-term care is staggeringly
expensive, and Medicaid winds up picking up most of the cost,
after recipients have spent down whatever they had planned to
leave to their heirs—or whatever their heirs had hoped to receive.
People who manage to stay out of institutional facilities in their
last ten or twenty years of life generally aren't "iterating" wealth.
While a small segment of the population—disproportionately
white, to be sure—may own wealth-generating assets such as
dividend-paying stocks or commercial real estate, by far the
majority of even moderately well-off people spend the last few
decades of life eating the fruits of their productive years, not nur-
turing cornucopias of generational wealth.

Higher rates of homeownership do correspond to both race
and wealth, somewhat axiomatically. Around 72 percent of whites
own their homes, against 44 percent of blacks, so it follows that
whites have higher average levels of net worth than blacks. But
the rub with having a substantial amount of your wealth tied up
in your house is that you can't liquidate it very easily, because you
still need to live somewhere. Selling your house for double what
you paid for it is great, but then you have to buy back into the
same housing market, unless you move to a cheaper and probably
less-desirable market.

This is why your house isn't really an investment in the way
that stocks or bonds or even gold are investments. It's like eval-
uating your wealth and thinking, *Well, I could always cash in my
vital organs on the transplant market.* Your house, like your lungs,
may have tremendous paper value, but it's not easy to trade on it.

People get rich from ownership of a primary residence
through a combination of timing and luck. If you bought a bun-
galow in Palo Alto in the mid-1980s and then sold it 40 years later,
when the market was high, to downsize and retire somewhere

else, you certainly would have done very well for yourself. You may walk away with several million dollars in cash and be able to live the rest of your life in comfort and have money to leave to your children. Or if you bought an abandoned brownstone on Avenue B in New York City's East Village or in Brooklyn's Park Slope in the late '70s for the tax debt, and fixed it up and lived in it, you could sell it today for a lot of money. There are many such people, and many of them are nonwhite.

But these are unusual cases. In reality, rich people have most of their wealth invested in nonresidential assets, and most home-owners don't see massive returns on their investment. In fact, between 2010 and 2020, 71 percent of the substantial increase in owner-occupied home value accrued to high-income house-holds.[27] Unsurprisingly, in an economy where the ultra-rich con-trol a growing percentage of the nation's wealth every decade, the amount of money they can demand for their homes in exclusive and coveted neighborhoods goes up as well.

Whites may have more aggregate wealth than blacks, but talking about "generational wealth" disguises the fact that few rich families actually hand down significant wealth for more than one or two generations. Most super-rich people in America did not inherit their money, and it is commonly said that 70 percent of wealthy families lose their money by the second generation, and 90 percent by the third generation. "From shirtsleeves to shirt-sleeves in three generations" is an old saying commonly attributed to Andrew Carnegie, and while it may or may not hold for every rich family, certainly many grand families of a century ago no lon-ger possess massive wealth. Inherited wealth tends to dissipate.

There's another point to be made about generational wealth, which is that intact two-parent households tend to be more effec-tive at generating wealth and passing it on. In 1970, 90 percent of white children lived in a two-parent household, while only 59 percent of black children were so fortunate. Those numbers got steadily worse for everyone, but black Americans were the worst affected. In 1994, only one-third of all black children lived with both parents, while more than three-quarters of white children lived in a two-parent household. It doesn't take a great deal of sociological analysis to understand that having one parent at home, as compared to two, generally equates to a lower standard of living and less wealth accumulation over time.

So, the Rothstein thesis that mortgage redlining by the government "caused" segregation and the disenfranchisement of African Americans is, predictably, limited and partial. Is it surprising to learn that black people during the Depression lived disproportionately in decrepit, unmortgageable houses in edge neighborhoods? Is it plausible that there were many racially mixed up-and-coming communities filled with houseproud blacks and whites that were stubbornly redlined in order to prevent black families from accruing assets?

The point of this book is not to defend the principle of dynastic wealth, celebrate the accomplishments of rich people, or argue that they deserve special respect. I am merely explaining that much of this talk about white "generational wealth" is nonsense and an excuse to come up with ways to enforce redistribution on a mass scale—like Communism but with race as a lever.

YES IN YOUR BACK YARD

A number of proposals to rectify the racial "property gap" have arisen in recent years. Possibly the boldest of these is reparations for slavery in the form of direct payments either to descendants of American slaves or to black people in general, or even to all nonwhite people. Laura Gomez, a law professor at the University of California, Los Angeles, wants the country to make financial and nonfinancial restitution to Latinos, for example. The state of California—where slavery never existed as a legal institution, though there were a few adventurers from the South during the Gold Rush who brought their slaves with them—established a commission to investigate the question of reparations.

"The modern racial wealth gap between African Americans and other racial groups began with enslavement," explains the 2022 Interim Report from the California Task Force to Study and Develop Reparation Proposals for African Americans. Paying the "slavery bill" demands careful calculation of back wages, the cost of human suffering, and a fair rate of interest that has accrued on all that money. The task force cites the work of German political scientist Thomas Craemer, whose "calculations for unpaid wages owed to enslaved people amounts to $19.4 trillion in today's dollars. He arrives at this number by multiplying the prevailing average market wage by the number of hours worked for each 24-hour day by those enslaved over the interval of 1776 to 1865 and applies a three percent interest rate." This modest figure of almost 20 trillion dollars is about two-thirds the American GDP and would represent a staggering increase in the national debt, not to mention the inflation surge from printing all that new money.[28]

But, as the report notes, 3 percent interest is measly compensation. "Merely doubling the interest rate to the more realistic six percent would increase the total estimate to $6.6 quadrillion in 2019 dollars."

Now we're talking! The total value of all assets on Earth is estimated to be around 500 trillion dollars, so the six or seven quadrillion dollars proposed to be paid to 50 million black Americans—roughly $130 million each—comes out to only 12 times the value of the entire world. This is the "more realistic" figure.

Another option, which some localities have begun to respond to, involves going back through property records, finding out if black people ever owned land that was lost to back taxes or eminent domain seizures, and demanding compensation for the descendants of the original owners. Manhattan Beach, a tony beachside town in Los Angeles County, recently ceded two parcels of land to the great-grandchildren of a black couple who had owned the land until 1927, when the county condemned the property—along with dozens of other parcels, mostly owned by whites. The two parcels of land were deeded to the descendants of the original owners, who sold the property back to the county for $20 million.

The primary effort over this century to address the racial wealth gap, and residential segregation in general, has been through the Fair Housing Act of 1968 (FHA) and the expansion and enforcement of its Affirmatively Furthering Fair Housing (AFFH) provision. The purpose of the FHA was to prevent discrimination in housing and gradually eliminate residential segregation. The AFFH aimed to address systemic issues like segregation, redlining, and exclusionary zoning, going beyond merely prohibiting overt discrimination. It required HUD and local governments receiving federal funds to actively promote integrated, equitable communities.

From 1968 to the 1990s, AFFH was weakly enforced. HUD required jurisdictions to certify compliance but lacked clear guidelines or rigorous oversight, leading to minimal action on desegregation. But under the Obama administration, and then again under Biden, the AFFH was strengthened. Jurisdictions had to conduct an Assessment of Fair Housing (AFH), using HUD-provided data to analyze housing segregation, discriminatory barriers, and "access to opportunity." The AFFH as reimagined by Obama/Biden, as critic Stanley Kurtz has astutely written, "is classic regulatory activism. It reads contemporary policy goals back into a law that mandated no such thing. AFFH, for example, slyly imposes a principle of 'economic integration' on the suburbs, although nowhere does U.S. law recognize or demand economic integration."[29]

"Fair housing," or "affordable housing," is a sneaky way for the Left to wage war on the suburbs that they see as racist, exploitative, environmentally unsustainable bastions of white supremacy. Social engineers can get away with a lot in the places and domains they control, such as major cities, large charitable foundations, universities, and newsrooms. But they run up against significant obstacles when they want to start changing the rules of how land is divided up and used. Most places in America are zoned by boards that are highly responsive to local public opinion, and Americans who own property are extraordinarily attuned to the factors that influence local quality of life and the value of their homes.

The typical modest suburb or bedroom community, at least for the sake of this argument, comprises several square miles of land that is platted or laid out to accommodate single-family homes of roughly 2,500 square feet, on a plot that is somewhere between 5,000 and 10,000 square feet, or one-tenth to one-fifth of an acre. The plot includes a driveway and room for two cars. Population density probably averages between 1,000 and 3,000 people per square mile. For comparison's sake, Manhattan has 75,000 people per square mile, Chicago has 12,000 people per square mile, and the city of Los Angeles has around 8,300 people per square mile.

As we discussed previously, the Left traditionally hates suburbs, aesthetically, politically, and morally. Suburbs are a breeding ground for conservative attitudes and foster irrational fear of outsiders. Suburbanites, frightened of any decline in the value of their homes, stymie the construction of new housing and stand in the way of needed progress. They are the ultimate NIMBYs, saying, "Put your low-income housing, battered women's shelters, apartment buildings, methadone clinics, commuter rail stations, and day-care centers anywhere you want, just *Not in My Back Yard*."

We are told constantly that America has a housing shortage, and that this is a major crisis. For instance, New York City is in such a perpetual state of emergency in regard to its more than two million rental units that rents have been regulated since World War II. The idea of an apartment shortage sounds dire, but while renting in many parts of the city can be a drag, there is no problem finding an apartment to rent if you are simply looking for a place to live and have some kind of salary approaching the area median household income. The real problem is that there is very little housing available for people who have no income or rely entirely on government benefits to get by.

So, it's not that there aren't enough literal housing units for Americans to inhabit. It's that there is a shortage of cheap housing, especially in places where people desire to live. Kirk McClure of the University of Kansas and Alex Schwartz of the New School conducted a deep 2024 study of housing vacancy rates across all 381 metropolitan areas and 561 "micropolitan" areas, finding that only a handful of areas were experiencing a housing shortage. "There is a commonly held belief that the United States has a shortage of housing. This can be found in the popular and academic literature and from the housing industry," McClure explained. "But the data shows that the majority of American markets have adequate supplies of housing available. Unfortunately, not enough of it is affordable, especially for low-income and very low-income families and individuals."[30]

On the other hand, we hear dire warnings about the housing crunch. "Economists estimate," says the *New York Times*, "that America needs between four million and eight million more homes." And the National Low-Income Housing Coalition agrees: "Nationally, there is a shortage of more than 7 million affordable homes for our nation's 10.8 million plus extremely low-income families." These numbers align with, and again speak to, the true nature of the crisis, which is the housing of very poor people, often single mothers with young children. The NLIHC repeats an alarming statistic, namely that, "there is no state or county where a renter working full-time at minimum wage can afford a two-bedroom apartment."[31]

This fact is often cited as evidence of the dismal, dystopian state of American capitalism. To think—a person who works full-time yet cannot afford a two-bedroom apartment! But very few full-time employees earn the minimum wage; the Bureau of Labor Statistics reports that only 1.1 percent of the workforce earns so little, and they skew young. In fact, almost half of the people who work for minimum wage are under 25 years old, and almost all are unmarried. Whether the minimum wage should be higher or not—and wages have certainly not kept up with worker productivity—it's not clear why the standard of minimum wage full-time work ought to be affording a two-bedroom apartment. Roughly half of people under 25 live with their parents.

Of course, it is true that working people in their twenties and thirties who would like to settle down, start a family, and begin climbing the "property ladder" by purchasing a starter home find themselves priced out of many markets. Though there was a great construction boom prior to the 2008 Great Recession, the crash in the market deterred builders from returning to the peak housing starts from the early years. Moreover, the houses they tended to build were higher-margin larger homes, like McMansions, priced beyond what young families could afford.

The housing expectations of young Americans have changed significantly from what their parents and grandparents were happy with. It's true that the average price of a house in 1975 was $43,000, or roughly three times the average household income, but that house was typically much smaller than the average house today. That $43,000 house was probably about 1,500 square feet, may have lacked central air conditioning, and likely had one or maybe two bathrooms. Houses today average 2,400 square feet and tend to have more amenities and features, driving up costs.

There are other factors that make it hard for people to find homes. Immigration certainly plays a role, though during the 2024 election campaign we heard economists rush to explain that adding five million or ten million adults to the country would have no impact on the availability or cost of housing. But that makes no sense, for when demand spikes but supply stays the same, how could the product not become scarcer or more expensive? In 2020 the country was flooded with trillions of dollars in cash when the government began sending out checks to every household and offering substantial grants or loans. The average cost of homes shot up 20 percent as large investors snapped up an estimated 15 percent of the country's housing stock.

In response to the supposed crisis of housing, a movement arose in the last ten or fifteen years that proudly refers to itself as YIMBY: "Yes In My Back Yard." The YIMBY movement began in San Francisco and spread nationally. It's based around the idea that what America needs is more residential building, of all kinds, immediately if not sooner, in order to "reduce poverty, end homelessness, eliminate racial segregation, create jobs, and stop climate change," according to YIMBY Action, an umbrella organization of local YIMBY groups. YIMBYs seek to "legalize housing," which is their way of demanding the elimination of local zoning laws that, for instance, permit only single-family housing within a given community or prevent people from subdividing

their three-bedroom house into a hostel with 15 small rooms to
rent to single adults.

YIMBY Action explains:

> American neighborhoods are defined by exclusion. Our
> system of exclusionary zoning bans duplexes, apartments,
> subsidized affordable housing, student housing and more
> in most "residential" areas. Excluding these types of
> residences keeps neighborhoods homogeneous and makes
> housing more expensive.
>
> YIMBYs advocate for the end of this ban on
> apartments and other kinds of housing; we want to end
> exclusionary zoning (aka "upzone").
>
> Upzoning is especially important in wealthy, high-
> opportunity neighborhoods where current zoning laws
> reinforce racial and class segregation.[32]

The politics of YIMBY are curious. Its rhetoric, as evidenced
above, is couched in blatantly leftist terminology about racial
and class segregation, and YIMBYs are explicit about wanting to
change radically the nature of suburbia as a kind of crusade. But
at the same time, their argument has deep libertarian implications: Why should a landowner be prevented from using his land
however he wishes? If I buy a house on a half-acre plot in a leafy
suburb, goes the argument, I should be allowed to build a twenty-
story 80-unit apartment building on it if I want to. That would
give hundreds of people a place to live rather than the single family of five who lived there before.

The mixture of leftist and libertarian politics defining
YIMBYism is confusing at first, until you remember that the
whole thing was cooked up in the Bay Area, home of the tech
revolution. Technocrats have always believed that society should

be controlled by experts who can manage things scientifically; the "tech bros" of today think similarly, only they microdose psychotropic drugs that inflate their self-confidence and bravado.

The same people who brought us the Metaverse (Mark Zuckerberg's stab at eliminating social life), Theranos (the celebrated but nonfunctioning blood-testing machine), and the Titan submersible (the doomed mini-submarine steered by a game console controller) brought us the YIMBY movement, which has the tech-inflected "move fast and break things" attitude, only applied to social policy and urban planning.

YIMBYism opposes the disproportionate power exercised by the "homevoter." The homevoter, as economist William A. Fischel explained in his 2001volume *The Homevoter Hypothesis*, represents the combined interests of homeowners to affect property taxes, zoning, and local spending. As Fischel writes:

> The homevoter hypothesis holds that homeowners, who are the most numerous and politically influential group within most localities, are guided by their concern for the value of their homes to make political decisions that are more efficient than those that would be made at a higher level of government. Homeowners are acutely aware that local amenities, public services, and taxes affect ("are capitalized in") the value of the largest single asset they own. As a result, they pay much closer attention to such policies at the local level than they would at the state or national level. They balance the benefits of local policies against the costs when the policies affect the value of their home, and they will tend to choose those policies that preserve or increase the value of their homes.[33]

From the perspective of renters or people looking to buy into a property market, homevoters have rigged the system against them. Why is it fair that San Francisco, which sits at the tip of a peninsula and thus has limited land for building out, has strict laws about building new housing or significantly altering the historic housing stock? Two-thirds of all the land in San Francisco is permitted for single-family housing only. The city, world-famous for its tens of thousands of picturesque Victorian houses known as the "painted ladies," disallows ("makes illegal") the construction of large apartment buildings across most of the city. And the pressure to keep the zoning laws as they are comes mostly from the homevoters who own those houses, who are strongly motivated by, and highly attuned to, any whiff of change that could impact local quality of life and the value of their houses.

Don't the homevoters understand that the young, the homeless, or people marooned in boring areas of the country, who don't have enough money to move, would also like to live in the Haight or Greenwich Village or Hawthorne Hills? Don't the residents of nice, appealing neighborhoods understand that if we were to raze them and build lots of thirty-five-story buildings with affordable apartments then *everyone* could enjoy living there?

The homevoter phenomenon occurs everywhere and is arguably at the core of the principle that "all politics is local." The YIMBY movement seeks to overcome the power of the homevoter by bypassing local zoning boards and taking their argument to the state level, where partisan legislators are more susceptible to arguments about the racial and economic justice implications of permitting more building, despite local zoning laws.

The YIMBY movement has succeeded in a number of jurisdictions. In 2019, the city of Minneapolis became the first in the nation to eliminate single-family zoning citywide, meaning that there is no bar in residentially zoned areas to building duplexes or triplexes. Minneapolis upzoned commercial corridors and areas near mass transit, permitting apartment buildings as high as thirty stories. The city removed all parking requirements for developers and reduced minimum lot sizes to encourage denser housing.

Oregon also eliminated single-family zoning in most cities statewide. Developers can now build quadruplexes in all residentially zoned areas. Washington State passed similar legislation in 2023, as have Montana and Idaho. In 2021, California passed the farthest-reaching such law, effectively eliminating single-family-only zoning in almost the entire state, with some exceptions. Efforts in New York State and Maryland—with their immensely rich and powerful suburbs—have made less headway.

This hardly sounds like the stuff of Communist revolution—a few triplexes in the neighborhood? An apartment building by the light rail station? And that's true enough. But you have to look beyond relatively anodyne changes in the zoning handbook to get at the real agenda.

When Barack Obama took office in 2009, he reconceptualized the way that cities interact with their surrounding areas. He brought a vision of *regionalism* to the city-suburb complex. As he told a gathering of mayors shortly after his first inauguration, "Yes, we need to fight poverty; yes, we need to fight crime. But we also need to stop seeing our cities as the problem and start seeing them as the solution. Because strong cities are the building blocks of strong regions, and strong regions are essential for a strong America."[34]

Decoded, what Obama envisioned was effectively an end to the splendid political isolation of the suburbs, and their integration with the cities around which they are built, and from which—in the words of the Brookings Institution—they unfairly "extract" their wealth. Obama's use of the Affirmatively Furthering Fair Housing rule was a broad effort to, in the words of Stanley Kurtz, "give the feds the ability to control local zoning regulations and

many other aspects of local government . . . not only by expanding central control but by turning suburban municipalities into
helpless satellites of neighboring urban centers."[35] The point was
to go beyond the Fair Housing Act—which outlawed racial discrimination in housing—and even go beyond trying to achieve
actual racial integration in housing. The goal for Obama and the
advocates was to achieve *economic* integration in American suburbs, and the vehicle for this program was forcing well-heeled
neighborhoods to *build*—not just permit, but actually build—
dense, low-income housing.

Much of this effort was informed by the work of Harvard
economist Raj Chetty, whose work famously suggested that "Zip
Code is destiny." Chetty used millions of IRS returns over time to
track intergenerational economic mobility; he determined that
your life opportunities are largely determined and defined by the
census tract you grew up in. This hypothesis has a simplicity to
it that appealed to opinion journalists and politicians: Children
who are raised in Evanston generally wind up better off than do
kids raised on the South Side of Chicago. This must be a question of resources. *Let's move the kids from Washington Park to the
Chicago suburbs, and they will soon be winning science fairs and
getting advanced degrees!*

One sees quickly that there is a massive confusion of cause
and effect going on here. It's certainly feasible that some kids
from an impoverished neighborhood would do better if they
were to live elsewhere. But evidence has shown that people tend
to bring their problems along with them when they move. Steve
Sailer has called Chetty's thesis an argument about "magic dirt vs.
tragic dirt."[36] Some places—like the South Bronx—are doomed
to produce poor outcomes, so removing people from that dys-
genic locale and replanting them in wholesome soil will inevi-
tably show improvement. But the original purpose of HUD was

to improve cities and make them better places for people to live, while ensuring that racism was not a factor in housing. HUD was never supposed to scatter poor people to rich areas and hope that proximity to well-off people would fix their problems.

Upon taking office in his first term, President Trump and his HUD Secretary Ben Carson undid Obama's AFFH rule; Biden reinstituted it, and Trump undid it again when he returned to office. Trump's 2024 campaign included strong rhetoric about the suburbs, which Democrats said was a racial "dog whistle," telling white women that their lily-white neighborhoods were about to be overrun by dusky hordes bearing housing vouchers, protected by government lawyers forcing their towns to sign consent decrees putting zoning decisions in the hands of some government bureaucrat. Which was kind of true.

But only kind of, because the suburbs today are not the suburbs that Malvina Reynolds sang about in 1962. Howard Husock, an astute housing critic, writes that the Obama-Biden AFFH worked "under a radical interpretation of the Fair Housing Act of 1968—one focused on ensuring that every community has a socio-economic mix rather than its facial goal: making sure that no household is denied housing it can afford to rent or buy. For HUD, it's as if we are still stuck in 1968, with the proposed rule even referencing that year's Kerner Commission report and its view that we are two nations, one white, one black."[37]

In reality, suburbs are where population and economic growth is happening across America, especially among nonwhites. In a recent analysis of 2020 Census data, Brookings reports that "a majority of major metro area residents in each race and ethnic group now lives in the suburbs. And for the first time, a majority of youth (under age 18) in these combined suburban areas is comprised of people of color." Black people have moved to suburbs in droves. In 1990, 37 percent of American blacks lived in suburbs; today, more than 54 percent of black people make their homes in suburbia. Across the country, "suburban populations are broadly diverse . . . all of the past decade's growth in big suburbs is attributable to people of color."[38]

The suburbs are also economically vibrant and are seeing the most general growth. Urbanist Joel Kotkin notes:

> In 1950, the core cities accounted for nearly 24 percent of the U.S. population; today the share is under 15 percent. In contrast, the suburbs and exurbs grew from housing 13 percent of the metropolitan population in 1940 to 86 percent in 2017—a gradual increase of 2 percent per year. Despite all the talk of moving "back to the city," commonplace for at least a generation, suburbs have accounted for about 90 percent of all U.S. metropolitan growth since 2010.
>
> Just as significantly, the suburbs and exurbs—once dismissed largely as "bedrooms" for core cities—now dominate job growth. From 2010 to 2017, over 80 percent of all job growth was in the suburbs and exurbs.[39]

All of this growth and vigor annoys the Left, which seeks to densify the American population, putting more people in less space. The Left hates "sprawl," which it characterizes as soulless and environmentally destructive. It limits sprawl through the imposition of green belts or urban edge boundaries—policies that curtail horizontal growth.

Density has its supporters. Many prominent urbanists, such as Edward Glaeser and Richard Florida, see dense living as fostering creativity and allowing for the promotion of thick social networks that drive innovation. Matthew Yglesias's 2020 book *One Billion Americans* and Ezra Klein and Derek Thompson's 2025 manifesto

Abundance are technocratic screeds about how the future of America lies in unleashing our native ingenuity, making housing legal again, and chasing growth like latter-day Babbitts. Some economists, mindful of criticism, encourage us to pursue "gentle density," which will preserve the "physical scale" of neighborhoods.

Gentle density is a fantasy. YIMBYs aren't worrying about densifying Utica, Baltimore, or Detroit. Those places are shrinking because there are no jobs there, and no one is moving there except for some urban homesteaders out for kicks. Densification is focused on places where people want to live, such as New York City and San Francisco, to name the two most obvious examples, though Boston, Washington, D.C., Los Angeles, and Atlanta are not far behind. "New York has a housing affordability crisis, and there's only one way out: build more housing," enthused Governor Hochul upon the 2023 passage of "City of Yes," a plan to build 80,000 new housing units in New York City over 15 years. But the city already builds between 25,000 and 30,000 units annually, and prices never come down. The dense gets denser.

Density is not really aimed at affordability. It is aimed at density. The Left adores density because, bluntly, cities vote Democrat. Conservative politics align with marriage and family, and the Left aims to discourage people from moving to the suburbs and exurbs, where they can spread out, put down roots, and consider having more than two children. It's no accident that, as Brookings notes, immigrants to the United States gravitate to suburbs, where they account for an astounding one-third of population growth.[40] People who schlep across the world to chase the "American Dream" do not fantasize of living in a crowded tenement or a repurposed shipping container, surrounded by the same people they are moving to get away from. They, like an increasing number of Americans, want a lawn, a house with multiple bedrooms, and space for two or more cars.

"Walkability" is a hot promise for the densifiers and was at the core of the "15-minute city" proposals that made the rounds at the height of Covid-related paranoia, when the Fauci-fanatics were planning to institute a global Big Reset. It's no mere coincidence that Carlos Moreno, the French-Colombian urbanist who devised the idea of the 15-minute city, was a member of the militant Communist terror group M-19 in Colombia at the height of its insurgency. The goal of the 15-minute city is to arrange life so that "people are no more than a 15-minute walk or bike ride away from all the services they need to live, learn, and thrive," in the words of a couple of optimists from the decidedly nondense precincts of the University of Woolongong in Australia.[41]

Erin Scronce, a senior World Bank external affairs officer, explains in a 2025 blog post on the World Bank website that she enjoys her life in suburban Virginia but has been "thinking about how cities are designed and what my life might be like if all the essentials—work, shopping, school, healthcare, entertainment—were just a short walk or bike ride away." Scronce compares two cities with comparable populations—Barcelona and Atlanta—and notes that Barcelona is 25 times as dense as Atlanta . . . and thus more "liveable."[42]

Scronce next praises Bogotá, Colombia; Dar es Salaam, Tanzania; and Quezon City, Philippines, as models of "transit-oriented development," which "prioritizes building dense, mixed-use neighborhoods that support and nourish public transport systems." But transit-oriented development and the creation of the 15-minute city "isn't just about reducing commute times; it's about rethinking how we live and interact with our cities."

So, if you want to know what kind of future the global elites have in mind for you, Mr. and Mrs. America, you need look no farther than those capstones of human-centered social life, Dar es Salaam and Quezon City!

The essence of the 15-minute city, if you hadn't noticed, is the elimination of the car. The Left hates cars; or rather, they hate *your* car, especially if it is gas-powered and allows you to disable the start/stop function when you are idling for more than five seconds. Making driving as expensive and cumbersome as possible is the keystone of the plan to force everyone to live stacked on top of one another. But cars are not just an impediment to the YIMBY vision—they are evil. Globalist organizations, like the World Bank, UNESCO, the World Economic Forum (whose formulation "You will own nothing and be happy" was the tagline of its Agenda 2030, a 17-point plan to establish "sustainable development" worldwide), and the Carnegie Endowment for International Peace, which invites us to develop "people-centered smart cities," all agree that the future will not be seen through the windshield of a car.

Environmental activist and author Rebecca Solnit is credited as saying, "the car has not only reshaped the physical landscape, but the moral one. It promised freedom, but often delivered dependence." Dependence, such as being able to go anywhere you want, whenever you want, and bring along your babies and elderly relatives, and their strollers and wheelchairs, too.

We are told that there is a fundamental opposition between "car-centric" and "people-centric" urban planning. But who drives cars? People. And why do they drive them? To go places.

Much of what urbanists propose regarding city planning is ultimately aimed at making cities as car-free as possible. Eliminating parking mandates in constructing apartments; closing thoroughfares to create pedestrian plazas; "daylighting" street corners by taking away spaces to provide for better lines of sight; the construction of endless bike lanes, which must be protected from cars by means of a buffer lane; lowering speed limits to 15 mph—these are the rational solutions to "traffic violence," formerly known as "accidents," and are the means to create people-oriented cities.

Pedestrian plazas and other forms of public space are a fetish of the bike-lane YIMBYist Left. When a city block is closed to traffic for a street fair or an "open streets" experiment, social media is flooded with pictures of children drawing chalk murals, and folk dancers demonstrating their steps where traffic normally flows. How wonderful: If only we were to stop subsidizing cars and instead repurpose all this precious urban space for human activity. But the grid of Manhattan, for example, with its wide streets and avenues perfect for the transportation of goods and people, was designed in 1811, long before the auto industry came along to reshape humanity along its nefarious ends.

Parks and public space are essential elements of city life. But public space in a dense conurbation only works if there are public trust, civility, respect for rules, and a robust police force to keep the peace. But you will be hard pressed to find a YIMBY activist who has a good word to say for law and order. They can't support the police, because the Defund movement is a cousin crusade. They both serve the same master.

All of the movements that I discuss in this book are related like this. I'm not saying it's a conspiracy, just that capturing these domains is essential to the victory of the Left. It helps to understand that YIMBY and open borders—as we had under Biden, and which the Left which would like to open again—are the same antidemocratic campaign. It's all a matter of establishing that the people who reside somewhere don't get a say in what happens there.

FOUR

EDUCATION

Pay Your Dues

One of Donald Trump's 2024 campaign promises echoed a long-sought dream of the American conservative movement, namely the abolition of the U.S. Department of Education (DoEd). Shortly after taking office for the second time, Trump issued an executive order to close the department in order to "return authority over education to the states and local communities."

The president is not permitted to shutter a major federal department unilaterally, but he can starve it of manpower and assign its functions to other agencies. The DoEd, though it commands a large budget, has relatively few employees, reflecting the fact that the department actually has little to do with running or managing America's 100,000 public schools. Out of a headcount of 4,133 employees at the DoEd, roughly 2,000 were let go through a combination of voluntary severance and a reduction in force

(RIF). In federal government employment terms, eliminating half a cabinet-level department's staff is basically unprecedented.

Outrage flowed from the educational establishment. Randi Weingarten, the powerful president of the American Federation of Teachers (AFT) and a significant power player in Democratic Party politics, fumed. "I'm mad. I'm spitting mad!" she told MSNBC. "The directive to 'return decision-making to the states' fails the smell test," Weingarten said in an AFT press release. "States and districts already govern schools through locally elected school boards, as they should. They put up most of the money and control most of the decisions—from approving curriculum to deciding who graduates."[1]

There is probably no issue in the life of everyday Americans where the tension between federal and local control is as starkly evident as in the domain of education. There are roughly 75 million students in America today, about two-thirds of whom attend public schools. Schools are most Americans' first introduction, upon entering their kindergarten classrooms, to state authority, in the imposing form of a teacher. Young adults may encounter government bureaucracy, arbitrary rule making, and absolute authority for the first time when they enroll their kids in school. School is an enormous source of anxiety for families and a huge contributing factor to real estate values.

While localities—as Weingarten acknowledges—exercise direct control over school district policies and curriculum, it's misleading to downplay the role of the federal government in education. Federal support amounts to about 10 percent of school funding nationwide and is frequently tied to adoption of the latest curricular fashion in education circles, as when the Obama administration dangled over $4 billion in "Race to the Top" school aid, contingent on adopting questionably rigorous "Common Core" standards and federally approved data collection methods. Though children—and even their parents—certainly aren't conscious of the federalist conflicts regarding school funding or bathroom gender policies, these tensions do underlie a lot of the daily reality of school in America.

The U.S. Constitution is silent on the question of education, which in the early days of the Republic was something of an ad hoc affair. In Puritan New England, smaller towns generally had elementary schools to teach boys and girls how to read and write, and larger towns also had grammar schools for talented well-off boys to learn Latin in preparation for careers as ministers or lawyers. Major cities had secondary schools. Very few people went to college. Apprenticeships were a common way for teenagers to become proficient in a trade. The federal government had little engagement in education, and following the Tenth Amendment left the question up to the states.

Public education as we know it today—free, compulsory, and universally accessible—emerged gradually in the United States over the nineteenth and early twentieth centuries. Horace Mann, often called the "father of American public education," pushed for a system of "common schools" that were publicly funded, nonsectarian, and open to all children. Mann was the consummate mid-nineteenth century New England social reformer and slavery abolitionist. His belief in the salvific power of education cannot be overstated; he famously remarked, "Education is our only political safety. Outside of this ark all is deluge."

Education was conceived of as a public good, not just a privilege for the elite; Mann convinced local worthies that taxes to train a literate future workforce would be well spent.

Massachusetts, under Mann's influence, passed a compulsory attendance law in 1852, setting a template for other states, which began passing compulsory education laws. These laws required children to attend school, whether public, private, or homeschool.

By 1900, about 31 states had such laws; Mississippi was the last to adopt the requirement in 1918.

High school became increasingly accessible in the early twentieth century, starting in Massachusetts and spreading outward. The construction of standalone high school buildings became a point of civic pride and marked the modern outlook of towns and counties that had them. High school education spread rapidly. In 1900, only 6 percent of the nation's teens graduated from high school, but by 1940 more than half were high school graduates.

Federal involvement in schooling remained minimal, though a failed congressional amendment in the 1870s laid the ground for future controversy. James Blaine, a Maine congressman, proposed to change the Constitution to ban states from using tax money to fund religious schools. Though the amendment failed in Congress, it led to similar laws in many states, amid anti-Irish sentiment, against funding parochial schools with public revenue.

In 1867, the government established an Office on Education, within the Department of the Interior. Though some reformers hoped to see a greater federal hand in public education through the operations of the office, it never became much more than a collector of data about educational institutions through the country, as well as a compiler of histories and brochures about state universities. This office persisted until 1979. Curiously, one of the motive forces behind the creation of the Office on Education was Zalmon Richards, another Massachusetts reformer who later became a cofounder and first president of the National Teachers Association, which eventually became the National Education Association, the massively powerful labor union that today counts some two million dues-paying members.

Federal involvement grew incrementally over the next century. The Morrill Acts of 1862 and 1890 provided for the creation of land-grant colleges with a technical and agricultural slant, which became the large state universities we know today. Along similar lines, recognizing the country's need for skilled technicians, Congress passed a national vocational education act in 1917, which funded secondary school education in "agriculture, trades and industry, and homemaking." With a federally derived funding stream, American vocational education became segregated from general education, a schism that persists to the present, and which some say has created an artificial division between college preparation and practical or technical know-how—perhaps to the detriment of the kids on both sides of that split.

Amid the flurry of major legislation that marked the presidency of Lyndon Johnson—the Civil Rights Act of 1964, the Voting Rights Act of 1965, the creation of Medicare and Medicaid in 1965, and the Immigration and Naturalization Act of 1965, among other consequential laws—the 1965 Elementary and Secondary Education Act (ESEA) can get overlooked. An important component of Johnson's War on Poverty, ESEA marked the first time that significant federal dollars, mostly earmarked for disadvantaged students, flowed to local school districts, setting the stage for direct federal involvement in local pedagogical practice.

Title I funding is directed specifically to poor school districts, but it comes with strings attached. States are required to adhere to federal rules on reporting, curriculum, spending, and standards in a manner that, to some critics, violates the federalist principles of the Founding, where each of the states is sovereign. The last sixty years have seen periodic flare-ups related to federal overreach versus local control of schools.

For example, in 1979 the Carter administration threatened to withhold Title I funding from Chicago if the city didn't actively desegregate its schools; this was taken to mean, and in fact meant, that the city would have to begin busing students out of their home districts in order to make the complexion of Chicago schools resemble the demographics of Chicago as a whole. This resulted in widespread protests, and Mayor Jane Byrne vowed not to implement wholesale busing.

"We've said from the beginning," Byrne explained, "that the neighborhood school system is what most families seem to prefer. . . . It would be very difficult for a child even to develop friendships if they're being shipped out of one community into another community." Asked whether busing would create "white flight" to suburbs or private schools, the mayor noted that with less than 20 percent white representation in the public schools, "there isn't a lot of flight left."[2]

This anecdote sums up six decades of push and pull that define local education under the lure and hook of federal funding. Neighborhood schools, family preferences, and children's friendships come into conflict with the racial gerrymandering obsessions of liberal law professors, judges, and Washington educrats. The principle of disparate impact meant that, from the perspective of a civil rights lawyer, any statistical deviation from an expected, race-neutral pattern could be defined as illegal segregation. The Civil Rights Act and its assorted penumbras and emanations gave courts astounding authority to impose orders on school districts to desegregate, and dozens of districts were sued by the federal government and forced to integrate their schools.

"Busing," as it came to be known, was among the hottest issues of the 1970s, when activists sought to integrate schools by forcibly transporting students into other districts or catchment areas. The U.S. Supreme Court ruled in its 1971 *Swann v. Charlotte-Mecklenburg* decision that it wasn't enough just to allow students to attend any school they wanted, regardless of race, but that districts had to take proactive steps to integrate the schools. This decision essentially gave judges around the country the power to impose busing to fix apparent racial segregation.

Busing was uniformly unpopular outside of the offices of the people who devised and imposed it. White and black people opposed it strongly, even while they expressed support for other measures aimed at racial integration of schools, such as redrawing school districts or building more low-income housing. Black students wound up being the ones who were more frequently bused into distant white schools, which meant they might spend an hour or more riding school buses each day. White parents worried that busing would erode community pride and cause discipline problems—not the most politically correct opinion, but probably legitimate anyway. Key Supreme Court rulings throughout the 1970s and '80s slowly drew back the power of judges to impose integration on school districts, and by the 1990s and early 2000s, most such efforts had ended.

It's true that American education is somewhat segregated, by fact if not by law. The trends are slowly changing. In 1995, according to Pew, about half of white students attended schools that were 90 percent white; by 2018, this number had dropped to just 18 percent of white students. For black students attending schools that are 90 percent black, the number has dropped from 22 percent in 1995 to 13 percent in 2018. Part of this has to do with more racial mixing in general, and also with the fact that the racial composition of the country is changing radically, especially among the younger segments. Whites simply aren't as dominant demographically as they were even a few decades ago.[3]

New York City's schools are deeply stratified by race, and many hard-left politicians campaign against the existence of what they call "apartheid schools." They want individual schools to match the racial composition of the city. But the demographics of the school-age population militate against this goal. Only 15 percent of the student body is white; even though the population of the city at large is 30 percent white, many white children attend private or religious schools. A large portion of white children live in places such as Staten Island or eastern Queens, which would mean that they would have to be bused across multiple boroughs in order to achieve the ideal balance. There's simply no way to achieve this goal politically.

And it's unclear why it's so important. Forced racial segregation is unquestionably bad for many reasons, but it doesn't follow that schools with few white students should necessarily be at an academic disadvantage. Is there something magical about sitting next to a white child that improves learning for nonwhite children? Most parents of all races want schools to provide a good education, regardless of their racial composition.

The demand for the racial gerrymandering of school districts in order to achieve parity is essentially ideological and only secondarily, if at all, concerned with educational outcomes for children. It also begs the question of why racial segregation persists seventy years after the *Brown* decision and sixty years after housing discrimination was made illegal at the federal level. Is it all driven by white supremacy?

Malcolm X spent most of his career as a minister for the Nation of Islam preaching in favor of racial separation and the diabolical nature of white people. But after he became a normal Muslim and participated in the pilgrimage to Mecca, shortly before he was murdered by members of the Nation of Islam, he forswore racism and embraced the principle of racial equality. However, he did not insist that people reject ethnic or racial identity. As he explains in his famous *Autobiography*:

> There was a color pattern in the huge crowds. Once I
> happened to notice this, I closely observed it thereafter.
> Being from America made me intensely sensitive to
> matters of color. I saw that people who looked alike

drew together and most of the time stayed together. This was entirely voluntary; there being no other reason for it. But Africans were with Africans. Pakistanis were with Pakistanis. And so on. I tucked it into my mind that when I returned home I would tell Americans this observation; that where true brotherhood existed among all colors, where no one felt segregated, where there was no "superiority" complex, no "inferiority" complex—then voluntarily, naturally, people of the same kind felt drawn together by that which they had in common.[4]

"Where true brotherhood existed . . . people of the same kind felt drawn together." Malcom X's disavowal of the cause of black divinity likely contributed to his assassination at the hands of his former fellow cultists in the Nation of Islam. While it might be stretching things to say that America today exists in a realm of "true brotherhood" among the races, one has to question the idea that racial statistical differences in schools or neighborhoods are necessarily evidence of ongoing white supremacist social structures, as opposed to being reflective of how people choose to live.

I asked a prominent black journalist about this one time. He indicated that the problem, from his perspective, was the cultural isolation of black children in schools that were almost entirely black. This makes a certain degree of sense and merits sympathy insofar as it acknowledges that African American urban culture is often characterized by intense dysfunction and needs help. One wonders whether mainstream society might be more open to forced integration efforts if it were explained as a matter of assisting our fellow Americans and less as an obligation borne of racial guilt.

Another key instance of the tension regarding local control of schools—with a different outcome—occurred in New York in the late 1960s. Changing demographics in Brooklyn led to certain neighborhoods, including Ocean Hill–Brownsville, shifting quickly from majority Jewish to majority black and Puerto Rican, mostly very poor. This resulted in extreme social dislocation and resentment, especially toward the public school system, which residents perceived to be racist.

In response to a citywide one-day boycott of school, the city Board of Education established three decentralized school districts, one of which was Ocean Hill–Brownsville. These districts were run by local, community-elected boards, which had the power to hire and fire principals and set curriculum. It was a test case for the Afrocentric idea of racial autonomy in black neighborhoods and the purported right of black students to have black teachers instruct them in black-oriented subjects using a black-friendly pedagogy.

One of the first actions of the new black superintendent of Ocean Hill–Brownsville was to fire 19 Jewish teachers and administrators. This move was highly popular in the community but angered the teachers union, the United Federation of Teachers (UFT), which had many Jewish members and threatened to go on strike unless the terminations were reversed. Ultimately, the teachers did walk out for seven weeks. Albert Shanker, the fiery leader of the UFT, went to jail for 15 days for violating the state's Taylor Law, which forbids public employees from striking.

The state education commissioner took over the Ocean Hill–Brownsville district and reinstated the dismissed teachers, ending the strike. But relations between the UFT and nonwhite communities across the city were soured. Shanker commented that "the whole alliance of liberals, blacks and Jews broke apart on this issue. It was a turning point in this way." The episode also hardened the teachers union against ideas of community control and in favor of tight centralization of school systems under the thumb of politicians who were dependent on the unions for votes and money.

Zohran Mamdani, incidentally, has indicated that he wants to end the system of mayoral control of the schools that has been in place since Michael Bloomberg wrenched it away from the local school boards in 2002. Mamdani says he wants to reform school control as a system of "cogovernance" with existing parent councils and school-level leadership teams. What this would likely mean is bringing the teachers union into near-direct control of the system.

Albert Shanker, the first president of the UFT, was a legendarily tough union leader in the style of labor bosses from earlier in the century. A funny line from Woody Allen's 1973 film *Sleeper* depicts a dystopian America hundreds of years in the future. Asked how the country was destroyed, an authority says, "Over a hundred years ago, a man named Albert Shanker got hold of a nuclear warhead." He is famous for having said, in response to a question about how certain negotiations would help children, "When schoolchildren start paying dues, that's when I'll start representing the interests of schoolchildren."

Shanker served as founder and president of the UFT from 1960 until 1986, and its mother organization, the American Federation of Teachers, from 1974 until his death in 1997. He was succeeded at the UFT and later AFT by his protégé Sandra Feldman, who in turn was succeeded at the UFT and later the AFT by Randi Weingarten, the Democrat Party power player who said she was "spitting mad" that President Trump was planning to dissolve the Department of Education.

The Department of Education was spun off from the Department of Health, Education, and Welfare (HEW) by Jimmy Carter in 1979, largely at the behest of the National Education Association (NEA), the sometime-rival union to the AFT. (The

NEA is larger than the AFT and focuses primarily on education policy advocacy, while the AFT is more oriented to fighting for labor rights and collective bargaining issues. The two organizations have considered merging at various points, and they effectively operate as partners.) The NEA made its first presidential endorsement in 1976, backing Carter, and raised significant funds for his campaign. This was the beginning of an unholy partnership between the teachers unions and the Democrat Party that has spanned half a century and raised, at a minimum, hundreds of millions of dollars in campaign contributions, virtually all of which has gone to Democrats.

The NEA pushed President Carter to establish the Department of Education in order to amplify their influence, secure more resources for public schools, and elevate their profession's status. Frustrated with the fragmented federal approach to education—programs scattered across agencies like Health, Education, and Welfare (HEW) lacked focus and clout—the AFT and NEA understood that a standalone department promised a direct line to federal power. Education was still largely funded at the state and local levels, but federal dollars were increasingly critical, especially after the 1965 Elementary and Secondary Education Act started funneling money to poor districts. The NEA believed a cabinet-level agency could lobby for bigger budgets.

But the unions' demand for a standalone cabinet-level department dedicated to federal supremacy in education was also based around a need for schooling to remain as it was—a publicly funded and publicly run institution with near monopoly power over teaching the tens of millions of children who would constantly enter the school system at one end and leave, twelve years later, at the other. The unions' interest in maintaining this monopoly was a question of power and of money. As long as teachers could be forced to pay dues to the union—a practice that was overturned by the Supreme Court in the 2018 *Janus* case—all that mattered was the flow of students and the funding that went with them. Preserving this flow became the raison d'être of the unions, and the Department of Education has been one of the unions' signs of power.

So, that helps to explain why Randi Weingarten is "spitting mad" about losing it.

FIGHT THE PARENTS!

In her 2025 book *Why Fascists Fear Teachers*, Randi Weingarten lays out "four foundational things that are important to the future of our students and the well-being of our nation—but are antithetical to the fascist anti-government, anti-pluralism, anti-opportunity agenda." Teachers "impart knowledge," Weingarten says, though this rather Prussian vision of pedagogy—children are vessels to be filled—has been passé at least since Rousseau, if not Plato. Teachers also "create safe and welcoming communities," and "opportunity."[5]

But the fourth "foundational thing" that teachers provide in the fight against fascism is that they are "anchors of a labor movement whose purpose is to champion the aspirations of working families." In other words, the teachers union isn't just how teachers get higher pay and job security; it's one of the reasons children attend school.

Randi Weingarten's professional and spiritual grandfather Albert Shanker may have been brutally transparent when he said he represents teachers, not children. But Weingarten has gone well beyond her predecessor, essentially saying that children go to school in order to keep teachers employed. Teachers aren't hired to teach students; children go to school because teachers are there.

The power of the teachers unions in American life cannot be overstated. With some 4.5 million combined members, the unions represent a massive voting block that is overwhelmingly left-leaning and Democrat-voting. The unions, along with their local affiliates, collect an estimated $2 billion in tax-exempt revenue annually, mostly through dues. Owing to the interlocking complexity of their organizations, it is hard to measure precisely how much money they spend on political contributions and lobbying, but reasonable estimates place the total amount spent by the national and local unions between $150 million and $300 million on each election cycle, on both electoral campaigns and ballot measures.[6]

That, plus millions of steely eyed, reliable voters, adds up to a lot of power and political access. Consider, for instance, the role that the teachers unions played during Covid in closing schools and then resisting their reopening. When the pandemic hit in March of 2020, teachers unions were quick to demand school closures, citing risks to teachers, staff, and students. The NEA and AFT issued statements urging districts to shut down and shift to remote learning.

In states with strong union bargaining power—like California, New York, and Illinois—unions negotiated with districts to ensure closures included paid leave and job protections. The UFT secured agreements for remote work. Even in nonbargaining states like Texas, unions like the Texas State Teachers Association lobbied governors to close schools, amplifying public health concerns. By April of 2020, nearly all U.S. schools—with teachers unions helping to formalize and sustain those decisions—were closed.

But as time went on, it became clear that kids weren't at great risk for getting Covid and certainly weren't dying from it. As pressure grew to reopen schools for the fall of 2020, unions pushed back hard, demanding strict safety protocols. Randi Weingarten called for "science-based" reopenings, insisting on masks, ventilation, distancing, and constant testing, even as some countries, like Sweden, kept schools open with fewer measures. The NEA issued a resolution tying reopenings to "near-zero" community transmission and full funding for safety upgrades, such as hospital-grade filtration systems, portable air purifiers in classrooms, daily deep cleaning of classrooms and bathrooms, and additional sanitation staff for each school. The Chicago Teachers Union (CTU) pushed for touchless faucets, soap dispensers, and hand sanitizer stations at every entrance and classroom.

The unions also demanded social distancing measures in all classrooms. Imposing six-foot distancing between students would require radical reconfiguration of school space and necessitate smaller class sizes—and more teachers. Class size reduction has always been at the top of the wish list for teachers unions and their advocates, who have claimed for years that smaller classes are the magic bullet for improving test scores and graduation rates, especially for black male students. With Covid, the unions finally had a compelling-sounding reason to hire more teachers and cut their workload: The Science demands it![7]

In the big blue cities, where public-sector unions rule the roost, the teachers flexed their muscles. In Chicago, the CTU staged a 2021 work stoppage, refusing in-person teaching until the city met its demands for testing and protective equipment. They won concessions, delaying full reopening until March of 2021. In Los Angeles, the teachers union pushed for remote-only instruction into 2021, citing inequities in low-income districts. Schools didn't fully reopen until April of 2021, even as private schools in the area resumed earlier. In New York, the UFT delayed fall 2020 reopenings twice, threatening strikes unless the city were to provide random testing and hybrid options. Partial reopenings dragged into 2021.

Teachers unions lobbied the CDC—the nation's public health agency—to fine-tune the agency's guidelines for reopening schools to keep it as slow as possible and carve out all manner of exceptions and accommodations based on local transmission rates, teacher vulnerability, or the presence in a teacher's home of someone with "high-risk conditions." AFT boss Randi Weingarten was in steady communication with CDC director Rochelle Walensky in the run-up to the February 2021 release of reopening guidelines, which were supposedly based on scientific data, not insider pressure. Multiple studies have demonstrated that districts with powerful teachers unions stayed remote on average 18 weeks longer in 2021 than other areas.

In a truly disgusting accusation, Randi Weingarten said that Jewish parents in urban areas who wanted schools to reopen were behaving like racist class traitors and enemies of the nonwhite poor. In a March 2021 interview with the Jewish Telegraphic Agency, Weingarten said:

> I have a very pointed response here for Jews making
> this argument.
>   American Jews are now part of the ownership class.
> Jews were immigrants from somewhere else. And they
> needed the right to have public education. And they
> needed power to have enough income and wealth for their
> families that they could put their kids through college
> and their kids could do better than they have done. Both
> economic opportunity through the labor movement and an
> educational opportunity through public education were key
> for Jews to go from the working class to the ownership class.
>   What I hear when I hear that question is that those who
> are in the ownership class now want to take that ladder of
> opportunity away from those who do not have it.[8]

So, wanting urban public schools to resume normal teaching was, according to the powerful president of a major teachers union, an attempt by the "ownership class" to "take the ladder of opportunity away" from lower-income people, even while the school closings had the worst and most disproportionate effect on poor, nonwhite children.[9] This argument is so perverse, and so illustrative of the thesis that teachers unions operate without regard for the welfare of children, that it is almost impossible to believe it wasn't made-up.

Why did the unions want to keep the schools closed? On one hand, it was like an extended vacation for teachers, who could conduct "remote instruction" over Zoom while driving their cars, lying in hammocks, or performing household chores. The UFT gave this multitasking a thumbs-up, cheerily noting that "teachers are working in many creative ways to provide instruction to their remote students."[10] But the unions were also holding public schoolchildren as hostages in their negotiations with the federal government for billions of dollars in Covid-related relief; the federal Education Stabilization Fund ultimately gave $250 billion to "prevent, prepare for, and respond to the coronavirus impacts on education for our nation's students."

The effects of the school closures on student achievement were dire. Prolonged remote learning led to substantial academic setbacks. The 2022 National Assessment of Educational Progress (NAEP) reported the largest declines in thirty years: fourth-grade math scores dropped five points, and reading fell three points. Eighth-grade math scores plummeted eight points.[11] Low-income and minority students were hit hardest. A 2021 McKinsey study estimated that black and Hispanic students had lost three to five months more learning than white students by the spring of 2021, widening achievement gaps.

The entire sense of the centrality of school to a child's daily existence was disrupted, and it's not clear that it will ever come back. After a year or more of virtual instruction, school has been redefined as a semivoluntary activity. Chronic absenteeism has almost doubled, and many more students have now experienced at least one year of extensive absence from school. The learning loss this represents is staggering, and the fallout will be felt for years. And while the teachers unions can't be blamed for Covid and its societal effects, the record is clear that they exploited the lockdown to achieve benefits for themselves at the expense of their students.

Maintaining and expanding the government's control over education facilitates the teachers unions control over the teachers and the schools, especially when Democrats are in power, but even when they aren't. While Republican presidents appoint incoming secretaries of education, the career staff of any executive department operate, as we have come to see, somewhat independently of their politically appointed bosses.

The idea of a "deep state" that runs the country isn't as mysteriously conspiratorial as it first sounded when the idea became current a decade ago. Since then, we have seen how a nexus of ideological allies across government, the media, academia, law, the "intelligence community," and nongovernmental public interest organizations operate as a kind of adjunct government, operating sometimes behind the scenes, sometimes right out front.

The organized efforts of this complex to obstruct and wreck Trump's first term in office brought its machinations to light. From the FBI's coordination with the 2016 Hillary Clinton campaign, the Obama presidency, and major law firms to spy on the Trump campaign, and then use friendly press sources to launder false information in order to justify further investigation, it became manifestly obvious to anyone who wasn't intentionally blinding themselves that our government wasn't operating as we had learned in civics class.

I have highlighted the role of the teachers unions in the formation of the Department of Education and in their ceaseless fight for resources to remain within the purview of the public education sector. But the teachers unions are not the only group within the Democrat/deep state superstructure that has an interest in the operation of the education system.

In May 2016, the secretaries of the Department of Justice and Department of Education issued a joint "Dear Colleague" letter directing public schools to allow transgender students to use the restrooms, locker rooms, and other sex-specific facilities that aligned with how they identified their gender rather than their sex "assigned at birth."[12]

Title IX of the 1972 Education Amendments bans discrimination on the basis of sex in schools receiving federal funding; the Obama administration, in this "Dear Colleague" guidance, interpreted Title IX as including gender identity. It specified that schools could not require medical diagnoses, treatments, or legal documents (like amended birth certificates) to recognize a student's gender identity. It also stated that "school staff and contractors will use pronouns and names consistent with a transgender student's gender identity." Though letters of this sort are not law, they are warnings that noncompliance will likely incur federal lawsuits.

This letter was likely a response to North Carolina's House Bill 2 (HB2), signed into law in March 2016, which mandated schools and state government facilities to restrict people to using the bathroom that matches their sex at birth. This bill ignited national fury and resulted in boycotts against North Carolina from around the country. The NBA moved its All-Star game out of the state, and the NCAA decided not to hold any of its playoff games there. North Carolina, facing enormous backlash, repealed the bathroom bill.

But the issue of the trans phenomenon was thorny and heated. Starting in the second Obama administration, the country was stunned as a form of social contagion called "rapid-onset gender dysphoria" swept the nation's junior high schools. Teenage girls, ever susceptible to peer pressure and fads, began insisting in great numbers that they were really boys caught in the wrong body. While puberty has always been a whipsaw experience during which children face serious questions about their identity, it has typically been the role of schools, doctors, the media, and the social services establishment to help kids manage the terrors of adolescence and early adulthood by letting them know that while their feelings are real, they can be dealt with and grown out of.

Some decades ago, there was a highly publicized epidemic of anorexia and bulimia among teenage girls. The response of the aforementioned authorities was to advise girls that society often values unrealistic beauty standards, that one's impressions of one-self in the mirror are not always accurate, and that there is treatment available for this disordered thinking. At no time was it the standard of care to take the anorexic girl's sense of being too fat seriously, and prescribe bariatric surgery so she would be unable to eat more than a spoonful of food.

But the epidemic of rapid onset gender dysphoria was handled differently. Not only were children who believed themselves to "really" be the opposite sex supposed to be taken seriously, parents were told that it was vital to rush their afflicted children into hormone therapy or even surgery before they committed suicide. "Would you rather have a dead daughter or a living son?" parents were asked. Putting ten-year-old children on puberty-blocking hormones was falsely characterized as a reversible "hold button" on the maturation process, as though human development is like a video that can be paused and restarted anytime, with no harm or stress on the equipment.

Public schools and unionized teachers stood in the forefront of culturing and encouraging trans delusions among children and passing laws to prevent their parents from finding out about it. At a 2022 House hearing on "anti-LGBT violence," Colorado social services executive Jessie Pocock was asked whether parents should be informed about what's going on with their children. Pocock told Congress that "those of us who are protecting and supporting young people are there and trusted with the information of the things that they are dealing with. In terms of parents' rights to know at schools, here in Colorado parents don't have the right . . . there are laws in place that say that [kids] have the right to process that with their trusted counselor."[13]

Pocock went on to say that "the age of consent to mental health therapy" on these matters in Colorado is twelve. These laws allow youth to connect with "trusted adults who can support them. That is so important; it prevents suicide." In some contexts, there is another name for people who represent themselves as "trusted adults" who advise confused young adolescents about their gender and sexuality, while warning them not to tell their parents.

A high-school teacher in Eau Claire, Wisconsin, hung a poster reading, "IF YOUR PARENTS AREN'T ACCEPTING OF YOUR IDENTITY I'M YOUR MOM NOW,"[14] with an image of a mama bear surrounded by her cubs. Other schools converted utility rooms or basements into "Gender Affirming Closets," funded by groups such as It Gets Better, a youth-focused LGBTQ+ advocacy organization praised by then-president Barack Obama in 2010. These special closets provide free access to makeup, breast binders, and "packers"—rubber phalluses for girls who want to appear to have a masculine bulge in their pants—to kids whose parents might not want to buy such paraphernalia.

Critics note that the broad promotion of trans messaging in schools goes beyond offering sympathy or understanding to struggling schoolchildren and crosses into advocacy for adopting a trans identity, even if this is putatively not the case. Programs like "Drag Queen Story Hour," where men, dressed up lavishly as extraordinary caricatures of women, read aloud from storybooks, are brought to schools and libraries throughout the country, often funded by local governments. The Drag Story Hour phenomenon became extraordinarily contentious, even when the drag performers did not oversexualize their performances, and the program has been blasted as a "grooming" mechanism for young children.

Advocates for Drag Queen Story Hour—and there are many—crack wise about the rubes who think that drag queens are coming for their kids, when all they want to do is come to a school or public library in full regalia, including outrageous wigs and absurdly high heels, and read a story to children who, according to the sponsors, adore seeing grown men dressed as grotesque parodies of women.

"I am proud," announced New York State Attorney General Letitia James, as she hosted a Drag Story Read-A-Thon at The Center, a well-known gay and lesbian community center in Greenwich Village, "to have been joined by my colleagues in advocacy and government today in celebration of the love, joy, and family fun that Drag Story Hour brings to our communities. Hate has no home in New York, and I will always fight to ensure our LGBTQ+ siblings' rights are upheld and defended." Then-Manhattan borough president New York City Comptroller Mark Levine praised the "messages of radical love and acceptance that characterize Drag Story Hour," and councilmember Tiffany Caban called it "a wonderful, wholesome, vital program."[15]

But what's the connection, exactly, between drag and literacy, much less between drag and children's entertainment? Drag is rooted in adult-oriented burlesque and nightclub routines and has been a raunchy element of gay culture for a century or more.

Children have never been an audience for drag, which exaggerates and pantomimes femininity with outrageous costumes, bawdy stage names, and outlandish makeup.

Indeed, there isn't even a clear connection between drag and homosexuality or transgenderism. One can argue that trans individuals are or are not incorrect about their gender, or believe that gay people are sinners, but in either case there are people in the world who have alternative gender and sexual identities.

But there are no drag queens in society. Unlike transgenderism or even a fetish like transvestism, drag is not an identity; it's a hobby. What is the lesson in tolerance that children are supposed to take away from being read to by a drag queen? There are, after all, straight drag performers (not "queens" per se) such as Milton Berle, Flip Wilson, Tyler Perry (despite rumors, apparently), and Barry Humphries ("Dame Edna")—maybe even homophobic ones.

Finally—and this is the crux of the issue—why only perform for children? There are a lot of people in society who might benefit from being read to. For instance, hospice patients or elderly people in rest homes would enjoy the company and might find the outfits amusing. Residents of homeless shelters, mental hospitals, and jails often have poor rates of literacy and could use some help with their reading, as could recently arrived migrants who need to get their English language skills up to speed. The fact that Drag Queen Story Hour is directed only at children is what gives the game away and deflates any argument that the program is not, in fact, a form of grooming.

Defending Education, a parents' rights group, reports that more than 1,200 school districts have policies that openly encourage personnel to keep a student's transgender status from their parents. These school districts educate more than twelve million students, or roughly one-quarter of the nation's public school population. The New York City Department of Education explains, "Sometimes transgender and gender expansive students begin their transition at school without a parent's knowledge."

> School staff must keep in mind that transgender and gender expansive youth may experience significant family challenges. Some transgender students have not talked to their parents about their gender identity and/or do not want their parents to know about their transgender status or gender expansive identity based on safety concerns or concerns about a lack of acceptance. These situations must be addressed on a case-by-case basis, accounting for the student's age and maturity, and will require schools to balance the goal of supporting the student with the requirement that parents be kept informed about their children. The most important consideration in such situations is the health and safety of the student.[16]

Accounting for the "health and safety of the student" in this context means keeping the parents in the dark. "The student is in charge of their gender transition and the school's role is to provide support. Where appropriate, the school administrator or another trusted adult"—that phrase again!—"in the school can meet with the student regarding their transition."

Robert Pondiscio, a former public school teacher, notes, "It is not possible to overstate the level of distrust, even contempt, reflected in the practice of excluding parents from discussions about their child's gender preference, even deceiving them if students claim their parents are unsupportive." Pondiscio also points out that teachers everywhere in America are "mandated reporters" who are legally required to alert the authorities if they suspect that kids are unsafe at home. "In no other conceivable instances is there any justification for excluding parents from profoundly life-altering decisions about their own children."[17]

The "contempt" that school authorities evidently have for parents was expressed dramatically in Loudoun County, Virginia, in 2021. In May of that year, a fifteen-year-old male student sexually assaulted a female classmate in a girls' bathroom at Stone Bridge High School. The attacker, who was wearing a skirt, arranged to meet the victim in the bathroom, where he raped her anally.

Though the attacker did not identify as trans, the fact that he was wearing a dress made the school district apprehensive of bad publicity, because the attack occurred while county administrators were thinking about establishing a policy allowing students to use the bathrooms matching their gender identity. School officials initially delayed reporting the incident to the Loudoun County Sheriff's Office, and the victim's parents were not immediately informed of the assault's nature.

Scott Smith, the victim's father, attended a school board meeting a month after the attack, where he was arrested for disorderly conduct after arguing with another parent, and getting—understandably—riled up about the topic of gender-fluid bathrooms. "My child was raped at school!" his wife shouted while Smith was being handcuffed. "And this is what happens!" District superintendent Scott Ziegler denied knowing anything about bathroom assaults, though he had been specifically informed about the rape. Then, adding insult to injury, the perpetrator was charged with forcible sodomy and transferred to a different high school, where he committed a second sexual assault in October of 2021.

A grand jury later found that the second assault could have been prevented, due to the district's inadequate response, including a lack of communication and failure to conduct a required Title IX investigation. Scott Ziegler was fired in December of 2022 following a grand jury report that criticized the district's "remarkable lack of curiosity" and prioritization of its own interests over student safety. The perpetrator was convicted of both assaults and sentenced to supervised probation in a residential treatment facility but was released in July of 2024, prompting further outrage from the victim's family.

The impression that much of the public took away from this bizarre incident was that the school administration in a large, wealthy Washington, D.C., bedroom community had covered up a rape by a male in a girls' bathroom because the news would have made it hard for the district to impose a "gender-expansive" policy regarding bathrooms and locker rooms. As former Wisconsin governor Scott Walker wrote, "It was clear that the school board and administrators were more concerned about furthering their transgender agenda than protecting the safety of students."[18]

The arrest and prosecution of Scott Smith—the father of the girl who was raped in the bathroom by a male sexual predator wearing a dress, after the county superintendent lied about his daughter's victimization—is not the only example of public-school administrators expressing contempt for the parents of the children they are hired to teach. Nicole Solas is a Rhode Island mother and attorney who was preparing to send her child to the local kindergarten in 2021. In speaking to the school's principal, Solas was surprised to learn that the teachers and administrators in the district did not use the outdated words "boy" and "girl" to describe their students, opting instead for gender-neutral terms and pronouns, and that politically charged lesson plans, pedagogy, and syllabi had infected the entire culture of teaching in the local system.

Solas asked to see the elementary school curriculum, which is legally public information, but her request was deferred by the principal, the school committee, the superintendent, and even the state department of education. Finally, she was told to submit a freedom of information request—in Rhode Island called an "Access to Public Records Act" (ARPA) request—to obtain the documents she wanted to review. But the district responded by telling her it would cost many tens of thousands of dollars to fulfill her ARPA request. The school committee even set an agenda item for a public meeting to discuss suing Solas for daring to bother them with so many requests.

It was obvious to anyone who bothered to pay attention that the school board wasn't really worried about the work involved in sending her the curriculum and emails pertaining to her questions; the scope of her request turned out to be perfectly legitimate. The real reason they were stonewalling was because they didn't want to reveal how deeply the district had waded into the swamp of critical race theory, gender studies, and the race communism that defines contemporary leftist politics.

Eventually the school district gave in to Solas and agreed to give her the information she wanted, with the usual redactions of personal information or other legally excludable matters. But then the local chapter of the National Education Association—the teachers union!—filed a lawsuit against Nicole Solas alleging that she was trying to get her hands on teachers' personal information, and demanded an injunction preventing the school committee from turning over the documents, or at least a substantial portion of them. It certainly appeared that the school administration and the NEA were colluding to prevent Solas—a local parent—from getting a peek at the corrosive educational stew they were dishing up.

As mentioned before, public-sector unions see every dollar of government expenditure not given to them as a kind of theft. That's pretty much the way the Left sees money, anyway. Listen to how they talk about tax cuts as a *cost*, when what's really happening is the state is taking less money from the people who made it. The Left's view of money is that it all belongs to the government, and people should be grateful for whatever amount they are allowed to keep.

Public schools educate about two-thirds of the nation's schoolchildren; the rest are in private or religious education or charter schools, or they are homeschooled. The Left believes that the state should have a monopoly on education, the same way the police exercise a monopoly on force, and fights vigorously to preserve it. Statists always think of children as a resource belonging to the public; parents may create them, but ultimately, they are property of the state. Maya Angelou, who famously recited a terrible poem at Bill Clinton's 1993 inauguration, is often quoted as saying, "Each child belongs to all of us," a statement that was echoed a few years later in the title of Hillary Clinton's 1996 book, *It Takes a Village*.

The idea that "It takes a village to raise a child," supposedly an African proverb though actually of uncertain origin, has great appeal for the matriarchal and socialist orientation of our contemporary pedagogical culture. It speaks to the decline of the traditional two-parent family structure and offers aid and comfort to the growing number of single-parent (typically mother-led) households with children. The centrality of government-sponsored child care as a campaign promise in Democrat Party politics should clue you in to the importance of the single mother in its voter base. Matthew Hennessey, a perceptive writer on faith, families, and American culture, notes, "progressives need reminders that their basic assumption about the relationship between citizens and the state is backward. Kids don't 'belong' to the government. They belong—if that's even the right word—to their families."[19]

In a word, the difference between the leftist vision of society and what might be called the conservative perspective comes down to the question of children and *whose* they are.

The public schooling advocacy complex wages war on educational alternatives. Following the pandemic, the number of students being homeschooled rose dramatically. In 2023, according to the Department of Education, 5.2 percent of students aged five to seventeen received instruction at home, versus 3.7 percent in 2019, though those numbers include students receiving full-time virtual education. Parents who homeschool typically expressed concern about the "environment" of regular schools, the desire to provide moral instruction, and dissatisfaction with academic instruction at traditional schools.

Homeschooling is particularly irksome to public school advocates because it implies that parents may be as capable as accredited educators at teaching children how to read, do math, and understand the world around them. Great efforts are made to suggest that homeschoolers are religious fanatics, apocalyptic "preppers," or illiterate racists. They have suggested that Adam Lanza, the perpetrator of the Sandy Hook school shooting, was a typical homeschooled child, when in fact the local school district had arranged for his "homebound" learning plan and failed to keep tabs on him, allowing him to graduate early. The massacre took place three years after Lanza had graduated; his many problems seem largely unrelated to his schooling.

Elizabeth Bartholet, a Harvard Law School professor and expert on civil rights and family law, has argued forcefully for a presumptive ban on homeschooling on the grounds that it poses a "danger to children and to society." According to Bartholet, homeschooling isolates children from the oversight of "mandated reporters," government agents, such as teachers, who are required to report suspicions of child abuse. "Teachers and other education personnel have long been responsible for a significant percentage of all reports to CPS, larger than any other group," reports Bartholet.

In addition to the children deprived of the loving eye of the surveillance state, "society loses out as well. Homeschooling presents both academic concerns and democratic concerns." Children who are homeschooled, says Bartholet, do not become productive adults capable of being employed, nor do they imbibe the "cultural values" that promote civic engagement. She explains:

> Many homeschooling parents are extreme ideologues, committed to raising their children within their belief systems isolated from any societal influence. Some believe that black people are inferior to white people and others that women should be subject to men and not educated for careers but instead raised to serve their fathers first and then their husbands. The danger is both to these children and to society. The children may not have the chance to choose for themselves whether to exit these ideological communities; society may not have the chance to teach them values important to the larger community, such as tolerance of other people's views and values.[20]

Bartholet acknowledges that there isn't a lot of evidence to back up her views about the disastrous outcomes afflicting homeschoolers, but she does point out that "many academics and the biggest teachers' unions in the country have found homeschooling deeply problematic." Regarding the sparse data buttressing her position, she says that's because "homeschoolers don't exist as a visible population due to the lack of regulation."

If America would only crack down on homeschooling families, investigate the parents, and conduct in-depth longitudinal studies on the children, then we could know for certain what a terrible job they are probably doing. Until then, we must rely on gut instinct that the homeschooled kids of today are the criminals and illiterates of tomorrow.

Religious education has long irked the forces of statism. As Randi Weingarten said in response to the possibility that the Supreme Court may permit religious charter schools to receive government funding, "public schools . . . are the bedrock of our democracy."[21] A major controversy in New York State has pitted two "competing interests" against one another: on one hand, the government's requirement that all children receive the right kind of education to make them into productive citizens in a pluralistic polity, and on the other, the right of parents to raise their children according to their own religious values.

New York has the nation's highest concentration of Jews, with almost two million Jewish New Yorkers statewide. Many members of this community are more or less completely integrated into secular society, and send their children to public schools, leaving religion for afternoons and weekends, or they forgo religious instruction entirely. Other Jews, desiring more religious education for their children, send them to private day schools that offer Hebrew-based instruction in addition to secular studies that are unquestionably as high-quality as anything in the public school system. These schools—called yeshivas—vary in the intensity of their religious training, but some are very rigorous.

There are, however, some ultra-Orthodox Hasidic Jewish communities—a very small percentage of the whole—that seek to educate their children maximally in Hebrew studies and place very little emphasis on secular learning, to the extent that, in some cases, they graduate from school scarcely speaking English, not being able to do math, and basically knowing nothing about America or the world they live in. I should add that this applies only to the boys of the community, who are meant to spend all their time studying Jewish law; the girls, who are not expected to study holy texts to the same extent, actually receive a better education in secular matters.

Reports that some yeshivas were not providing an education that was "substantially equivalent" to that of their peers in public schools scandalized New York's social service busybodies and other self-declared watchdogs. The *New York Times* fervently embraced the issue of yeshiva curricula, running a dozen or more lengthy analyses of the Hasidic schools over seven years, along with repeated editorials. "The schools," explained the paper of record in 2022, "appear to be operating in violation of state laws that guarantee children an adequate education. Even so, the *Times* found, the Hasidic boys' schools have found ways of tapping into enormous sums of government money, collecting more than $1 billion in the past four years alone."[22]

All religious schools in New York State receive public money to pay for meals, transportation, nonreligious books, and other items, including assistance for special education students. One billion dollars sounds like a lot, even over four years, though the fact that the state spends $89 billion on education annually puts that figure into perspective, as does the fact that there are 65,000 yeshiva students; the "billion dollars" comes out to $3,800 per yeshiva student per year, or less than one-tenth the amount spent on students in the public system.

Though acknowledging that the problem of total failure to teach secular subjects was limited to just a handful of yeshivas, the *Times* reports that students at "the Central United Talmudical Academy agreed to give state standardized tests in reading and math to more than 1,000 students. Every one of them failed." Indeed, that sounds pretty bad . . . but compared to what?

The New York City public schools are extraordinarily well funded, at slightly more than $42,000 per student, or close to double the national average. And while many of the city's schools are excellent, a great many others are subpar, to say the least.

The gold standard for the testing of American schoolchildren is the National Assessment of Educational Progress. The 2024 results for New York City were sobering. "Overall, just 33 percent of the city's fourth graders scored proficient in math last year. . . . Of the city's eighth graders, 23 percent scored proficient in math and 29 percent scored proficient in reading. . . . Meanwhile, 28 percent of the city's fourth graders scored proficient in reading."[23] Compared to the rest of the country, New York is paying filet mignon prices for beef heart performance. "New York's fourth grade students rank 32nd and 46th on reading and math NAEP exams, respectively, while eighth grade students rank 9th and 22nd."[24]

Well, defenders of the public schools might retort, that's a lot better than the worst yeshivas. That's true, but it misses the whole point, which is that the yeshivas aren't *trying* to do well on the tests, whereas that's literally the main objective of public schools. The tightly knit Hasidic communities that support the yeshivas and populate their classrooms reject the premise of modern education—to prepare young people to become productive members of society and "to teach them values important to the larger community" as Elizabeth Bartholet suggests—in favor of the values that matter most to them.

What are those values? Simply put, to produce more Hasidim and preserve the continuity of the community. You can find this an absurd perspective. You can suggest that it does a disservice to the community's children for whom entering American secular society is made difficult. You can insist—quite reasonably—that the schools that fail to offer even rudimentary instruction in English subjects not receive any state funding. (This is happening: New York has cut off a handful of particularly egregious yeshivas.) But at the same time, we have to acknowledge that American liberty and its freedom of conscience preserve the right of families to raise their children—and this freedom, while not absolute, is broad.

A series of U.S. Supreme Court cases throughout the twentieth century established firmly that the care and raising of children is the responsibility of the parents, and the state's interest in the child's welfare is limited to ensuring its health and safety, that is, preventing actual child abuse. In *Pierce v. Society of Sisters* (1925), the Court held that "the fundamental theory of liberty upon which all governments in this Union repose excludes any general power of the State to standardize its children by forcing them to accept instruction from public teachers only."

The rejection of "standardizing" children by subjecting them all to the same type of schooling sounds like something modern, out of Pink Floyd's *The Wall* (e.g., "We don't need no education/ We don't need no thought control. . . ."), so it's curious to see how antithetical the idea of pedagogical uniformity is to the American spirit of liberty, even a century ago.

The Court continued in *Pierce*, in which Oregon tried to mandate public school for all children, "the child is not the mere creature of the State." This is a key point that came up 75 years later, in *Troxel v. Granville* (2000), which was not an education case but dealt with a Washington state law providing for third-party rights to visit children over the objection of the parent. It's worth quoting at length:

> The interest of parents in the care, custody, and control of their children is perhaps the oldest of the fundamental liberty interests recognized by this Court.
>
> In light of this extensive precedent, it cannot now be doubted that the Due Process Clause of the Fourteenth Amendment protects the fundamental right of parents to make decisions concerning the care, custody, and control of their children. . . .

> The Due Process Clause does not permit a State to
> infringe on the fundamental right of parents to make
> childrearing decisions simply because a state judge believes
> a "better" decision could be made.[25]

This expansive understanding of parental rights as virtually total certainly conflicts with the "It takes a village" theory of child-rearing, or author James Baldwin's oft-cited assertion that "The children are always ours, every single one of them, all over the globe."[26] That's not to say that we don't cherish and love all children, and want the best for them, and want to take care of orphans, or children who are sick or hungry. But children are made by their parents, not as future taxpayers or soldiers or consumers or voters, but as members of a family, which is the first social unit that children are aware of and has always been the matrix of the individual.

The yeshivas in New York that do a terrible job in educating children in English and mathematics—though it really must be emphasized that these few schools are not representative of even ultra-Orthodox Jewish schools—are a kind of limit case for American religious liberty. The Amish are similar. Amish schools run through eighth grade and are taught by Amish girls with an eighth-grade education. But that's the way the Amish have organized their communities, and their right to do so was affirmed by the U.S. Supreme Court in *Wisconsin v. Yoder* (1970), which held that "the history and culture of Western civilization reflect a strong tradition of parental concern for the nurture and upbringing of their children. This primary role of the parents in the upbringing of their children is now established beyond debate as an enduring American tradition."[27]

We may find it odious and insane to raise children in a strict religious environment where they don't even learn the basics of

American history or even the national language. But the point of religious liberty isn't tolerance of religion that doesn't annoy you. Just as with speech, it's the religious practices that seem completely at odds with the mainstream that need protection.

And to return briefly to the question of the public schools—the union-run schools—how well are they preparing American youth for the workforce and to be well-informed self-governing subjects of our Republic?

Not that well, it turns out. Given the amount of money America spends per pupil, we are decidedly mediocre. The PISA test (Program for International Student Assessment) assesses fifteen-year-olds on their reading, math, and science literacy. It is given in dozens of countries every three years and is widely considered a reliable measurement. PISA scores put American students decidedly in the middle of the pack. Among the other participating Organization for Economic Cooperation and Development (OECD) nations, U.S. students underperform every Asian country and most European countries in math, and do moderately well in reading and science literacy.

But PISA is too broad a measure to assess the relative quality of public, union-run schools in America. Fortunately we can drill down to look at how well charter schools perform against union-run "district schools," specifically in those districts where the teachers unions are very powerful. Charter schools are typically government-funded, not-for-profit public schools that operate semiautonomously; there are some for-profit charter schools, but only in a few jurisdictions, and many states ban them outright.

Charters grew out of the school choice movement, which sought to give families more options regarding their children's education through state-issued vouchers representing the per-pupil cost of tuition. Reformers argued that letting a thousand pedagogical flowers bloom would give vent to teachers' creativity; economists contended that increased competition would encourage poorly performing schools to do better, lifting all boats. Ironically, even Albert Shanker, then the president of the AFT, backed charter schools as an opportunity for teachers to break free of onerous rules.

When the first charters—so called because they operate under a "charter" from their jurisdiction—opened their doors in the 1990s, they were an immediate hit with families eager for an alternative to their local traditional public school. Over the last thirty years, charters have spread widely across the country. There are roughly 8,000 charter schools, educating around four million students. About 7 percent of all public-school students attend charter schools.

With so many charter schools, operating across 46 states, obviously there will be differences in quality. But generally speaking, charter schools outperform their traditional public-school counterparts. A 2023 study by Stanford University's Center for Research on Education Outcomes (CREDO) found that, in regard to progress throughout a given school year, "in math, charter school students, on average, advanced their learning by an additional six days in a year's time, and in reading added 16 days of learning."[28] Given that the school year is typically 180 days, those imputed extra days of learning are astonishingly significant.

But when you drill down, the improvements are staggering. In New York City, charter students achieved a 42-day advance in reading proficiency over district schools; charter schools across New York State as a whole had a 75-day advantage. Rhode Island—where the union sued a mother who tried to get curricular information—saw its charter schools outperform district schools by 90 days in reading. Similar numbers held in math. Illinois charter students, for instance, gained a 48-day advantage over their district school counterparts. The gains are strongest, unsurprisingly, in poorer areas.

The CREDO report explains, "This growth represents accelerated learning gains for tens of thousands of students across the country. Each student and each school is a proof point that shows that it is possible to change the trajectory of learning for students at scale, and it is possible to dramatically accelerate growth for students who have traditionally been underserved by traditional school systems."

Naturally enough, powerful teachers unions, anxious about competition to their monopoly, have fought to stop the expansion of charter schools. Most charter schools are nonunion, raising ostensible concerns about teacher job security, pay, and working conditions; more realistically, unions also worry about district schools losing funding. As charters grew more popular, union resistance intensified. The AFT and NEA argued that charters undermined public education by "creaming" high-performing students, leaving traditional schools with higher-needs populations and less funding.

This argument, that high-demanding charters flunk out or expel low-performing students, sending them back to the district schools as the classroom-of-last-resort, is reminiscent of an *Onion* parody news segment. A panel of experts debates the question, "Are Tests Biased Against Students Who Don't Give a Shit?" A new study by the Department of Education, we are told in the satirical bit, finds that "students who think school is a boring waste of time score significantly lower on their standardized tests than their peers."[29]

Obviously, this is just a joke, but it contains an important truth within it. Charter schools attract kids whose parents are invested in their children's education; it is well established that parental involvement is a predictor of educational success. Children will respond to positive stimulation, whether in district schools or charter schools, but their precious class time is wasted when teachers must attend to disciplinary hard cases for half the period.

Maybe it's unfair that the district schools get saddled with a disproportionate number of unmotivated children while the charters get to "cream" or "cherry pick" the one whose parents bothered to apply, but where does that leave the kids who want to learn and who have strong support at home? Should their education suffer because a couple of bad apples take up all the oxygen in the room? Under President George W. Bush the federal government pushed a program called "No Child Left Behind." But another way of looking at that approach could be called "No Child Gets Ahead."

Ever since the charter movement took flight and demonstrated successful outcomes, teachers unions have turned against them. In New York City, charter schools educate roughly 18 percent of the city's public school students—remember, charters are public schools, operating independently of the Department of Education. Ninety percent of charter school students in New York are black or Latino, 82 percent of them are from economically disadvantaged families, and one-in-five has an Individualized Education Program (IEP), which is indicated when a student has a disability. So, the argument that charter schools are creaming the student population doesn't hold up.

But the United Federation of Teachers has waged a frantic war against the expansion of charter schools, even though there is a long waiting list of families who are eager to enroll their children. New York State maintains a cap on the number of charter schools that are allowed to open, and the UFT fights doggedly to keep the cap on tight. Michael Mulgrew, head of the UFT, says that "Corporate charter chains drain space, money and resources from public schools and our students bear the cost," and that charter schools "drain the lifeblood from public schools."[30] But what he calls "corporate" charter chains are not-for-profit networks that run a number of charter schools based on an effective method. They are "corporate" in the same way that New York City has a "corporation counsel" that represents the city in legal matters.

In Chicago, Mayor Brandon Johnson is a former public-school teacher and Chicago Teachers Union organizer. Johnson ran for office with explicit promises to back the CTU, and to fund schools based on "need" rather than "enrollment." Enrollment-based funding is based on a formula; need-based funding is highly subjective and open to interpretation. Johnson's negotiations with the CTU on the teachers' contract was a stunning example of institutional capture. Even *Labor Notes*, a prominent pro-union magazine, was taken aback by how expansively the city of Chicago—in terrible fiscal shape—had bowed to the demands of the CTU. "The new contract addresses both bread and butter concerns and common-good demands. Said CTU president Stacy Davis Gates, a member of the union's Caucus of Rank and File Educators: 'It was the whole buffet.'"[31]

Johnson, as mayor, has fought charter schools with all the focus one would expect of a professional teachers union organizer. He decries the "harm that sustained disinvestment has on Chicago's communities and youth." He claims that he has worked too long for the public schools to see black children hurt by charter schools. Meanwhile, charter schools in Chicago almost entirely serve black children, who significantly outperform their peers at traditional neighborhood schools.

The spirit of Albert Shanker, who said that he would start representing the interests of schoolchildren when schoolchildren start paying union dues, presides in union-run school districts across America. There are many excellent public-school teachers, and people who go into teaching generally want to help children develop into intelligent, productive adults. But organized labor, which has no business in the domain of public-sector employment, has captured public education and would prefer to destroy the futures of America's youth than concede control of significant tax revenue.

The Left, when you get down to it, has little interest in education, in the sense of leading young people to discover knowledge, learn about the world, and spark the spirit of inquiry. Oh, it likes the vast sums of *money* involved, and the power that comes from controlling it and having access to so many little minds to mold.

Individual teachers may have serious commitment to their students, at least at first, but in my experience, if you speak to any civil servant for 15 minutes, they will start talking about how many years they have until they can retire and start collecting a pension.

The problem with education for the Left is that success in school is based on individual merit, hard work, and self-discipline. There's really no way around this. But what do grit and smarts have to do with an agenda of equality of outcome, communal guilt and racial debt, and undoing systemic global oppression? If the goal of the Left is to get tomorrow's voters on board with gender fluidity, green politics, and the destruction of the West, then encouraging them to go home, shut out all distractions, and hit the books is a form of counter-messaging.

So, that's the sense in which the Left have "weaponized" education: They marched through and captured the institution over decades, unionized it, and leveraged its members' dues into an electoral slush fund. The Left gained control of curricular development, increasingly froze out parents, and surreptitiously, in the name of kindness and antibullying initiatives, turned school into an indoctrination center for radical perspectives on gender and privilege.

CONCLUSION

People have asked me what I mean when I talk about "the Left" in this book. Who are they, and what do they want?

One December, some years back, one of my children came home from grade school and said, "We have to write a report about a New Year's resolution for the world." More or less like: *What is something that the whole world should resolve to do, or do better, in the coming year?* She wanted a suggestion.

"Everyone should mind their business," I suggested. "That way, nobody would bother anyone else."

She looked at me. "I don't think that's the sort of thing they were talking about."

Well, of course not. School—especially a public school in upper Manhattan—is really not about self-reliance, temperance, discipline, or any of the other Puritan virtues that fed Benjamin Franklin, who had his favorite motto, "MIND YOUR BUSINESS," stamped onto America's first circulated coin, the 1787 Fugio cent.

Minding your business is a funny thing. On one hand, it means how people mean it, namely "Mind your own business," but it also means "Mind your p's and q's," "Stick to your knitting," "Cobbler, to thy last," or any of the dozens of sayings counseling prudence and low time-preference that any American of a certain age grew up hearing.

Essentially, I see the Left as inveterately incapable of minding its business. You know the old saw about politics, the one the Left is forever repeating? "You may not be interested in politics, but politics is interested in you."

The Right always disregards this sentiment, thinking, *Well I don't care if it's interested in me; I'm still not interested.* The Left like it, because they love politics, they love the idea that it's interested in them, they aren't surprised, because they know how fascinating they are, and because they identify so strongly with politics that they consider it their right to be interested in you and so to mind your business.

I guess, roughly speaking, the Left includes everyone who is interested in poking in other people's business.

That's probably a bit overbroad. But even though I live in New York City and work in journalism, I am fond of the type of cantankerous Yankee who essentially wants to be left alone. Like the neighbor in "Mending Wall": *Good fences make good neighbors.*

As I said earlier, it helps to consider the idea that YIMBY and open borders stem from the same impulse: The belief that the people who live somewhere aren't the ones who get to decide what happens there.

Weaponization of our fundamental institutions is how the Left destroys what remains of America.

NOTES

Chapter One

1. https://www.heritage.org/border-security/commentary/stop
   -allowing-noncitizens-determine-congressional-and-presidential
2. https://www.justice.gov/usao-ndca/pr/jose-inez-garcia-zarate
   -pleads-guilty-federal-firearm-charges-death-kate-steinle
3. https://time.com/3923128/donald-trump-announcement-speech/
4. https://www.nytimes.com/2015/07/13/opinion/lost-in-the
   -immigration-frenzy.html
5. https://www.politico.com/magazine/story/2017/12/06/kate-steinle
   -murder-trial-jury-didnt-botch-216016/
6. https://www.kqed.org/news/11633296/steinle-trial-verdict#:
7. https://www.themarshallproject.org/2019/12/12/i-did-my-25-years
   -now-i-m-fighting-another-sentence-deportation
8. https://www.marinatimes.com/the-mansion-that-fentanyl-built
9. https://nida.nih.gov/research-topics/trends-statistics/overdose
   -death-rates#Fig3
10. https://www.nytimes.com/2018/01/29/nyregion/judge-released
    -immigrant-ragbir.html
11. https://clarke.house.gov/clarke-releases-statement-on-bidens-pardon
    -of-immigrant-rights-advocate-ravi-ragbir/
12. https://www.guardian.co.tt/news/161-venezuelans-deported-over-2
    -days-by-national-security-ministry-6.2.1883075.ccbdb86d3f
13. https://x.com/KamalaHarris/status/825117135794008064
14. https://x.com/abhiandniyu/status/1969293219230802218
15. https://www.nbcnews.com/world/asia/h1-b-visa-fee-crushes
    -american-dream-indian-students-rcna234640
16. https://x.com/AnnCoulter/status/1955257751166243188

217

17. https://news.gallup.com/poll/391820/four-americans-highly
    -concerned-illegal-immigration.aspx
18. https://today.yougov.com/politics/articles/49083-how-americans
    -want-the-government-to-handle-the-issues-that-matter-most-to
    -them
19. https://www.youtube.com/watch?v=g1xdYcYxhFA
20. https://iaproject.org/cdn/resources/reports/US_Commission_
    Immigration_Reform_Barbara_Jordan.pdf
21. Eugene McCarthy, *A Colony of the World* (Hippocrene Books, 1992),
    p. 1.
22. https://www.heritage.org/immigration/report/assessing-the-trump
    -administrations-immigration-policies
23. https://jewishreviewofbooks.com/articles/3169/in-the-melting-pot/
24. https://www.presidency.ucsb.edu/documents/remarks-kennedy
    -lawrence-dinner-pittsburgh-pennsylvania
25. https://ia801301.us.archive.org/33/items/in.ernet.dli.2015.130942/
    2015.130942.A-Nation-Of-Immigrants_text.pdf
26. https://americanhistory.si.edu/becoming-us/sites/default/files/case
    -study/downloads/HartCeller%20readings%20and%20handouts.pdf
27. https://files.eportfolios.macaulay.cuny.edu/wp-content/uploads/
    sites/4886/2015/01/16060742/cis.org-Three_Decades_of_Mass_
    Immigration_The_Legacy_of_the_1965_Immigration_Act.pdf
28. https://cis.org/Report/Legacy-1965-Immigration-Act
29. https://www.pewresearch.org/race-and-ethnicity/2015/09/28/
    chapter-2-immigrations-impact-on-past-and-future-u-s-population
    -change/#:~:text=The%20nation's%20population%20grew%20by,are
    %20their%20children%20or%20grandchildren
30. https://cis.org/Report/Legacy-1965-Immigration-Act
31. https://www.unz.com/isteve/will-the-zeroth-amendment-trump-the
    -first-amendment/
32. https://www.presidency.ucsb.edu/documents/hillary-clinton-campaign
    -press-release-hillary-clinton-gave-major-speech-immigration-heres
33. https://obamawhitehouse.archives.gov/the-press-office/2012/07/04/
    remarks-president-naturalization-ceremony
34. https://www.gilderlehrman.org/history-resources/teacher-resources/
    statistics-trends-american-farming
35. https://nces.ed.gov/programs/digest/d17/tables/dt17_219.10.asp#:
    ~:text=The%20primary%20purpose%20of%20the%20Digest%20

of,both%20government%20and%20private%2C%20and%20draws
%20especially

36. https://www.loc.gov/classroom-materials/immigration/italian/the
    -great-arrival/#:~:text=This%20new%20generation%20of%20Italian,
    they%20were%20known%20as%20ritornati
37. https://www.youtube.com/watch?v=Jmov6EjlZLU
38. https://x.com/SpeakerPelosi/status/1399828572563517440
39. https://www.rollingstone.com/politics/politics-features/why-border
    -walls-dont-work-782449/
40. https://www.brookings.edu/blog/order-from-chaos/2015/09/15/
    something-there-is-that-doesnt-love-a-wall-mexico-and-the-u-s
    -presidential-campaign/
41. https://www.nytimes.com/2016/07/29/us/politics/convention
    -highlights.html
42. https://www.texastribune.org/?p=114157
43. https://www.justice.gov/usao-mn/pr/federal-jury-finds-feeding-our
    -future-mastermind-and-co-defendant-guilty-250-million
44. https://www.legistorm.com/stormfeed/view_rss/530378/
    member/835/title/ellison-paulsen-duffy-applaud-passage-of-money
    -remittances-improvement-act.html
45. https://www.sctimes.com/story/news/local/2015/10/13/gov-dayton
    -provides-harsh-criticism-racial-tensions/73836696/
46. https://www.npr.org/2022/05/16/1099034094/what-is-the-great
    -replacement-theory
47. https://www.nytimes.com/2018/10/29/opinion/stacey-abrams
    -georgia-governor-election-brian-kemp.html
48. https://news.yahoo.com/senate-democratic-whip-claims-demographics
    -232124671.html
49. https://www.mediamatters.org/media/3971581
50. https://www.uscis.gov/sites/default/files/document/data/h-1b
    -petitions-by-gender-country-of-birth-fy2019.pdf
51. https://www.epi.org/publication/congressional-immigration
    -reforms-needed-to-protect-skilled-american-workers/
52. https://x.com/VivekGRamaswamy/status/1872312139945234507
    ?lang=en
53. https://americanmind.org/salvo/thats-not-happening-and-its-good
    -that-it-is/

Chapter Two

1. https://www.presidency.ucsb.edu/documents/keynote-address-the
   -2004-democratic-national-convention
2. https://www.npr.org/2008/03/18/88478467/transcript-barack-obamas
   -speech-on-race
3. Ibram X. Kendi, *How to Be an Antiracist* (One World, 2023), Chapter 1.
4. https://www.nytimes.com/2020/06/04/us/floyd-memorial-funeral.html
5. https://americanmind.org/salvo/the-scapegoating-of-derek-chauvin
   -pt-i/
6. https://x.com/RepBowman/status/1619363897701720065
7. https://www.cnn.com/2023/01/27/opinions/tyre-nichols-memphis
   -police-department-jones
8. https://www.nytimes.com/2019/10/26/opinion/new-jersey-high
   -school-racism.html
9. https://council.nyc.gov/carlina-rivera/2025/03/10/amny-i-am
   -fearful-immigrants-at-east-village-church-voice-angst-and-anger
   -over-ice-raids-and-whether-theyre-next-to-be-targeted/
10. https://naacp.org/find-resources/history-explained/origins-modern
    -day-policing
11. https://x.com/RashidaTlaib/status/1381745303997534216
12. https://www.youtube.com/watch?v=uZpGjyX7Pqg
13. https://ocasio-cortez.house.gov/media/in-the-news/alexandria
    -ocasio-cortez-was-asked-about-defunding-police-and-her-answer
    -went
14. https://now.tufts.edu/2020/06/17/how-racial-segregation-and
    -policing-intersect-america
15. https://council.nyc.gov/press/wp-content/uploads/sites/56/2025/03/
    2025-State-of-the-City-Remarks.pdf
16. https://www.theatlantic.com/politics/archive/2017/12/the
    -criminalization-of-gentrifying-neighborhoods/548837/
17. https://www.cssny.org/news/entry/New-Neighbors
18. https://www.city-journal.org/article/our-latest-karen
19. https://x.com/CabanD22/status/1574416545131945985
20. https://x.com/CabanD22/status/1574826993258041347
21. https://righttobe.org/guides/bystander-intervention-training/
22. https://www.cbsnews.com/newyork/news/citi-bike-fight-video
    -woman-attorney/
23. https://pjmedia.com/benbartee/2023/05/24/watch-bike-karen-race
    -hoaxers-flee-like-hunted-rats-to-avoid-lawsuit-n1697819

24. Ruby Hamad, *White Tears/Brown Scars* (Catapult, 2020), p. 4.
25. Robin DiAngelo, *White Fragility* (Beacon Press, 2022), p. 2.
26. https://manhattan.institute/article/perceptions-are-not-reality-what-americans-get-wrong-about-police-violence
27. https://www.washingtonpost.com/graphics/investigations/police-shootings-database/
28. https://ucr.fbi.gov/crime-in-the-u.s/2019/crime-in-the-u.s.-2019/topic-pages/tables/table-43
29. Alex Vitale, *The End of Policing* (Verso, 2021), p. 222.
30. https://grabien.com/story?id=533660
31. Frantz Fanon, *The Wretched of the Earth* (Grove Press, 1963), p. 74.
32. https://www.marxists.org/archive/khrushchev/1956/02/24.htm
33. George Jackson, *Soledad Brother: The Prison Letters of George Jackson* (Lawrence Hill Books, 1994), pp. 309–310.
34. https://jonestown.sdsu.edu/?page_id=19027
35. https://www.cadtm.org/spip.php?page=imprimer&id_article=14451
36. Angela Davis, *Are Prisons Obsolete?* (Seven Stories Press, 2003), p. 27.
37. https://www.theatlantic.com/politics/archive/2016/03/hillary-clinton-intersectionality/472872/
38. https://afsc.org/stop-cop-city-campaign
39. https://citylimits.org/opinion-mayor-adams-wants-to-turn-nyc-into-cop-city/
40. https://www.theguardian.com/us-news/article/2024/may/13/cop-city-emory-atlanta-israel
41. https://x.com/mazemoore/status/1982974662175752646
42. https://www.presidency.ucsb.edu/documents/letter-the-resolution-federation-federal-employees-against-strikes-federal-service
43. https://www.bls.gov/news.release/pdf/union2.pdf
44. https://projects.propublica.org/nonprofits/organizations/383652741/202003149349304370/full
45. https://x.com/ammaralijan/status/1936499606772498635
46. https://chicago.suntimes.com/madigan-trial-news/2024/12/04/mike-madigan-corruption-trial-u-s-rep-nikki-budzinski-testify
47. https://x.com/Brandon4Chicago/status/1801259760529895606
48. https://x.com/thehill/status/1282358303549464578?s=20
49. https://lsupress.org/do-hard-times-cause-crime-the-lessons-of-history/#:~:text=The%20Great%20Depression%20of%20the,worst%20years%20of%20the%20Depression

50. https://www.vera.org/publications/investing-in-evidence-based
-alternatives-to-policing

51. https://theintercept.com/2018/04/11/saheed-vassell-brooklyn
-gentrification-nypd/

52. https://x.com/MayorJenny/status/1271226762198835205

53. https://jimowles.org/news/candidate-answers-to-joldc-gale-brewer
-for-city-council-district-6

54. https://opportunityagenda.org/toa-toolkit/

55. https://oag.dc.gov/public-safety/cure-streets-oags-violence
-interruption-program

56. https://www.justice.gov/usao-dc/pr/convicted-drive-shooting-and
-fentanyl-trafficking-member-21st-and-vietnam-crew-sentenced

57. https://mpdc.dc.gov/release/mpd-makes-two-arrests-2023-nightclub
-homicide

58. https://lasentinel.net/governor-signs-jones-sawyers-ab-413-the-at
-promise-youth-bill.html

59. https://codes.findlaw.com/ca/education-code/edc-sect-54690/

Chapter Three

1. https://www.fhfa.gov/news/statement/fhfa-director-sandra-l.
-thompsons-statement-on-upfront-fees-based-on-certain-borrowers
-debt-to

2. https://www.federalregister.gov/documents/2021/01/25/2021-01753/
advancing-racial-equity-and-support-for-underserved-communities
-through-the-federal-government

3. https://www.facebook.com/KamalaHarris/videos/equity/1731574083
660306/

4. https://heretohome.org/covenant/

5. For a deep analysis of how the Civil Rights Era represented the
introduction of a new regime co-existing with the foundational
Constitutional order, see Christopher Caldwell's seminal *The Age of
Entitlement: America Since the Sixties* (Simon & Schuster, 2020).

6. https://www.reaganlibrary.gov/archives/speech/remarks-signing-bill
-making-birthday-martin-luther-king-jr-national-holiday

7. Christopher Caldwell, *The Age of Entitlement: America Since the
Sixties* (Simon & Schuster, 2020) p. 41.

8. https://byrdlab.sites.ucsc.edu/microreport/

9. https://www.nytimes.com/2020/07/15/style/jane-elliott-anti-racism
.html

10. https://www.newyorker.com/news/the-new-yorker-interview/pete
    -buttigieg-plans-win-democratic-presidential-nomination-defeat
    -trump
11. https://www.minneapolisfed.org/article/2022/how-the-racial-wealth
    -gap-has-evolved-and-why-it-persists
12. https://www.thenation.com/article/society/target-pride-suburbs
    -fascism/
13. https://nlihc.org/resource/myth-white-suburb-and-suburban
    -invasion
14. https://www.cnn.com/2019/10/30/politics/michelle-obama-white
    -flight
15. https://prospect.org/2011/03/28/crime-white-flight-racial-anxiety/
16. https://www.city-journal.org/article/the-truth-about-white-flight
17. https://www.commentary.org/articles/norman-podhoretz/my-negro
    -problem-and-ours/
18. https://cdn.vanderbilt.edu/vu-wordpress-0/wp-content/uploads/
    sites/278/2020/10/19115823/White-Mens-Roads-Through-Black
    -Mens-Homes-Advancing-Racial-Equity-Through-Highway
    -Reconstruction.pdf
19. https://www.bloomberg.com/graphics/2021-urban-highways
    -infrastructure-racism/
20. Tom Lewis, *Divided Highways* (Cornell, 2013), p. 122.
21. https://www.brookings.edu/articles/homeownership-racial
    -segregation-and-policies-for-racial-wealth-equity/
22. https://nypost.com/2019/01/10/de-blasio-theres-plenty-of-money
    -in-nyc-its-just-in-the-wrong-hands/
23. https://www.americanprogress.org/article/eliminating-black-white
    -wealth-gap-generational-challenge/
24. https://www.federalreserve.gov/econresdata/feds/2015/files/2015076
    pap.pdf
25. https://www.supremecourt.gov/opinions/22pdf/20-1199_hgdj.pdf
26. https://budgetmodel.wharton.upenn.edu/issues/2021/12/17/
    inheritances-by-race
27. https://www.housingwire.com/articles/homeowners-gain-8-2-trillion
    -in-housing-wealth-over-10-years/
28. https://oag.ca.gov/ab3121/report
29. https://www.nationalreview.com/corner/affh-has-no-basis-fair-housing
    -act/

30. https://www.tandfonline.com/doi/full/10.1080/10511482.2024
    .2334011?src=exp-la
31. https://nlihc.org/explore-issues/why-we-care/problem
32. https://new.yimbyaction.org/solutions/
33. William Fischel, *The Homevoter Hypothesis* (Harvard University
    Press, 2005), p. 4.
34. https://www.presidency.ucsb.edu/documents/remarks-the-us
    -conference-mayors-miami-florida
35. https://eppc.org/publication/trump-kills-an-intrusive-housing-rule
    -again/
36. https://www.unz.com/isteve/the-atlantic-whites-turned-the-magic
    -dirt-into-tragic-dirt/
37. https://www.aei.org/op-eds/citing-equity-biden-revives-a-pernicious
    -housing-proposal-from-the-obama-administration/
38. https://www.brookings.edu/articles/todays-suburbs-are-symbolic-of
    -americas-rising-diversity-a-2020-census-portrait/#:~:text=While%
    20there%20is%20still%20a,2000%20and%2045%25%20in%202020
39. https://americanmind.org/features/the-rise-and-fall-of-new-york/
    ex-urbia/
40. https://www.brookings.edu/articles/immigration-and-poverty-in
    -americas-suburbs/
41. https://theconversation.com/forget-the-conspiracies-15-minute
    -cities-will-free-us-to-improve-our-mental-health-and-wellbeing
    -200823
42. https://blogs.worldbank.org/en/transport/the-15-minute-city

Chapter Four

1. https://www.aft.org/press-release/afts-weingarten-trumps-order
   -dismantle-education-department
2. https://mdh.contentdm.oclc.org/digital/collection/colmo7/id/207405/
3. https://www.pewresearch.org/short-reads/2021/12/15/u-s-public
   -school-students-often-go-to-schools-where-at-least-half-of-their
   -peers-are-the-same-race-or-ethnicity/#:~:text=Among%20Black%
   20students%2C%20the%20share,42%25%20in%202018%2D2019
4. Malcolm X, *The Autobiography of Malcolm X* (Ballantine, 1990), p. 395.
5. Randi Weingarten, *Why Fascists Fear Teachers* (Thesis, 2025), p. 12.
6. https://commonwealthfoundation.org/research/government-unions
   -fund-politics/
7. https://classsizematters.org/wp-content/uploads/2011/04/CSR_
   Black-Male-Outcomes-Report-3.18.pdf

8. https://www.bnaibrith.org/jewish-groups-blast-incendiary-remark
   -by-teachers-union-head-calling-us-jews-part-of-ownership-class
   -over-school-reopening-debate-html/
9. https://www.aecf.org/blog/pandemic-learning-loss-impacting-young
   -peoples-futures
10. https://nypost.com/2020/11/07/nyc-conduct-remote-lessons-from
    -hammocks-moving-cars/
11. https://www.edweek.org/leadership/two-decades-of-progress-nearly
    -gone-national-math-reading-scores-hit-historic-lows/2022/10
12. https://www.justice.gov/opa/file/850986/dl?inline=
13. https://www.congress.gov/117/meeting/house/115243/witnesses/
    HHRG-117-GO00-Wstate-PocockJ-20221214.pdf
14. https://www.newsweek.com/sign-telling-identity-confused-kids-im
    -your-mom-now-sparks-controversy-1685713
15. https://ag.ny.gov/press-release/2023/attorney-general-james-hosts
    -drag-story-hour-read-thon-new-york-city
16. https://www.schools.nyc.gov/school-life/school-environment/
    guidelines-on-gender/guidelines-to-support-transgender-and
    -gender-expansive-students
17. https://fordhaminstitute.org/national/commentary/hill-public
    -education-dies-transgender-policies-utter-contempt-parents
18. https://www.washingtontimes.com/news/2022/mar/18/transgender
    -indoctrination-our-nations-schools/
19. https://www.wsj.com/opinion/the-never-ending-war-on-home-schooling
    -blame-education-b383064b?mod=Searchresults&pos=3&page=1
20. https://news.harvard.edu/gazette/story/2020/05/law-school
    -professor-says-there-may-be-a-dark-side-of-homeschooling/
21. https://www.aft.org/press-release/afts-weingarten-us-supreme-court
    -decision-religious-charter-school-case
22. https://www.nytimes.com/2022/09/11/nyregion/hasidic-yeshivas
    -schools-new-york.html
23. https://www.chalkbeat.org/newyork/2025/01/29/naep-scores-show
    -recovery-in-nyc-fourth-grade-math-as-reading-holds-steady/
24. https://cbcny.org/research/highest-costs-middling-marks
25. https://supreme.justia.com/cases/federal/us/530/57/
26. https://www.thenation.com/article/archive/notes-house-bondage/
27. https://supreme.justia.com/cases/federal/us/406/205/
28. https://ncss3.stanford.edu/executive-summary/full-executive
    -summary/

29. https://theonion.com/in-the-know-are-tests-biased-against-students
    -who-dont-1819594957/
30. https://www.uft.org/news/press-releases/uft-president-michael
    -mulgrew-reacts-chancellor-david-banks-policy-address#:~:text=
    In%20response%2C%20UFT%20(%20United%20Federation%20
    of,President%20Michael%20Mulgrew%20issued%20the%20
    following%20statement
31. https://labornotes.org/2025/04/chicago-teachers-approve-contract
    -remarkable-gains

ACKNOWLEDGMENTS

I have a lot of people to thank. My wife, for starters, was very patient with me while I worked on this project. Pat Dixon reminded me that writing this was something I *get* to do, not something I *have* to do. Paul Beston gave me encouragement. Subject-matter experts Stephen Eide, Nicole Gelinas, Aaron Renn, Chris Caldwell, Joel Kotkin, Emmett Hare, Howard Husock, and Bill Voegeli all gave me valuable insights, tips, and suggestions.

Jason Blum is always a fount of wisdom, and he was unsparing with his assistance. Lance Duerfahrd's words of warning rang in my ears. Kenin Spivak gave me careful counsel, and Alan Astro provided a low, constant hum of nervous energy that buoyed me.

Elroy gave me the perspective of today's Communist youth. Blake showed me the importance of keeping one's back to the goal.

Chris Ruddy and Keith Pfeffer, my publisher and editor at Humanix, were extremely patient. Mary Glenn pushed me to come up with an idea for the book. My agent, Frank Weimann, got the whole thing going.

My dad was always helpful. My children are themselves, which is all I wanted.

INDEX

232 INDEX

236   INDEX

Khrushchev, Nikita, 84, 85
King, Martin Luther, Jr., 65,
   125–129
Klein, Ezra, 167–168
Kotkin, Joel, 167
Kropotkin, Peter, 78
Kurtz, Stanley, 156–157
Kuswa, Kevin, 142

Labor force:
   1900 to 1920, 32–33
   at current time, 34
   and H-1B visas, 18, 50–54
   impact of immigration on, 55
   minimum wage workers in,
      159
   and patronage system, 100–101
   safety advancements in, 79
   schools' preparation of youth
      for, 208
   threat of immigration to,
      22–23, 25
   (See also Unions)
Labor market, mass immigration
   and, 18–19
Labor Notes, 212
Land grant colleges, 176–177
Lanza, Adam, 201
Latzer, Barry, 109
Law and order, purpose of, 78–80
Law enforcement:
   in effort to destroy Trump, xviii
   for illegal aliens, 3–5, 9
   for immigration, 19–20, 37–38
   weaponization of, xvi
   (See also Public safety)
Lazarus, Emma, 39
Left:
   and Christian moralism, 59
   conspiracies essential to, 171
   Davis as éminence grise of, 91
   enthymemic reasoning by,
      94–95, 109

"equality" replaced with "equity"
   by, 122
minding of others› business by,
   215–216
and "national interest" debate,
   25
"public safety" hijacked by, 72
on residential segregation, 133
   (See also Housing)
value system of, 127
view of cars by, 170–171
view of money by, 199
vision of children in society
   among, 200–201
war against local communities
   by, 132
weaponization of key
   institutions by, xviii–xix (See
   also individual institutions)
white racial guilt exploited by,
   76
Lenin, Vladimir, 92, 94
Lennon, John, 88, 90
Levine, Mark, 194
Lewinsky, Monica, xvi
Lewis, Sinclair, 137
Lewis, Tom, 146
Lightfoot, Lori, 42, 107
"Little Boxes" (Reynolds), 137–138

Madigan, Michael, 107
MAGA movement, xvii–xviii,
   59–60
Make the Road, 105–106
Malcolm X, 180–181
Mamdani, Zohran:
   on calling police, 73
   on control of schools, 183
   groups supporting, 104, 105
   on police/policing, 94, 95, 99,
      110
   political stance of, 83
   on violence, 79

ABOUT
THE AUTHOR

SETH BARRON is on the editorial board of the *New York Post* and is a New York City-based reporter and editor who has covered local and national politics closely for many years. His work has appeared in the *New York Post, New York Daily News, Wall Street Journal*, and *Tablet*. He frequently appears on a range of local and national television and radio programs as a commentator. Barron is the author of *The Last Days of New York: A Reporter's True Tale*, of which NEWSMAX host Greg Kelly wrote: "Barron cuts through the noise and provides a devastating account of a city's decline under the delusional leadership of socialists and con men."